I AM FIFTY,
AND I DON'T
WANT TO DIE

A Mum's Struggle to Overcome Her
Addiction to Codeine Painkillers

ABBY LIVERINGHOUSE

BALBOA.
PRESS
A DIVISION OF HAY HOUSE

This is a true story. To protect the privacy of individuals, names, locations, and identifying details such as occupations and places of residence have been changed. All names are false to hide these individuals' identities.

Balboa Press books may be ordered through booksellers or by contacting:

Balboa Press
A Division of Hay House
1663 Liberty Drive
Bloomington, IN 47403
www.balboapress.com.au
1 (877) 407-4847

Because of the dynamic nature of the Internet, any web addresses or links contained in this book may have changed since publication and may no longer be valid. The views expressed in this work are solely those of the author and do not necessarily reflect the views of the publisher, and the publisher hereby disclaims any responsibility for them.

The author of this book does not dispense medical advice or prescribe the use of any technique as a form of treatment for physical, emotional, or medical problems without the advice of a physician, either directly or indirectly. The intent of the author is only to offer information of a general nature to help you in your quest for emotional and spiritual well-being. In the event you use any of the information in this book for yourself, which is your constitutional right, the author and the publisher assume no responsibility for your actions.

Any people depicted in stock imagery provided by Thinkstock are models, and such images are being used for illustrative purposes only. Certain stock imagery © Thinkstock.

Print information available on the last page.

ISBN: 978-1-5043-0272-2 (sc)
ISBN: 978-1-5043-0273-9 (e)

Balboa Press rev. date: 06/08/2016

INTRODUCTION

IN THE ENGLISH SUMMER OF 2014, a lonely police worker was found dead in her apartment following an overdose of illegal drugs containing cocaine, amphetamines, and ecstasy. The woman, who was in her mid-thirties, had become addicted to a common brand of analgesics containing codeine. This codeine-based painkiller can be obtained over the counter (without a doctor's prescription) in Great Britain, Australia, and New Zealand.

The woman had become depressed after the tragedy of her father's death in a car crash a few years earlier, followed by a relationship breakdown. She also suffered from chronic back pain and migraines due to a fall down a flight of stairs. According to her mother and sister, she was prone to stress, anxiety, and depression. Over a period of fifteen years, she became addicted to codeine-based painkillers, taking thirty to forty tablets a day. She tried to stop taking the over-the-counter analgesic several times without success.

In 2010, she took part in a methadone substitution programme to try and wean her off this substance, but she couldn't break her habit. In the end, she went as far as begging local pharmacists not to sell her the medication anymore. In spite of this desperate measure, she relapsed and drove long distances to nearby villages to obtain these tablets. Nothing helped, and the woman became discouraged at her failed attempts to give up the drug.

While her friends began settling down and having children, she continued to do shift work in the police force, which prevented her from having a normal routine or a satisfying social life. She became increasingly isolated as she drifted away from her friends. Feeling left out was another reason she found it difficult to break her addiction.

In the beginning, her addiction was probably an attempt to obliterate psychological pain due to unresolved grief. A lot of people become hooked on over-the-counter painkillers to relieve stress and anxiety. For this woman, it was a way to cope with pressure at work and in her private life, as well as a remedy for physical pain, especially after her fall down the stairs.

The mystery surrounding her death was never solved. No one figured out why she resorted to illegal drugs in the end. Did she take them regularly, or was it the first time? Was her final overdose intentional? Perhaps she was so desperate, so unhappy with herself for not being able to stop taking painkillers that she decided to take her own life with a cocktail of illicit drugs.

When I found this story on the Internet, I felt sad and scared. I could relate to this woman's plight. Blessed with a beautiful family, I am fortunate not to be lonely like she was. But I could relate to her stresses, having to do shift work, as well as her feelings of anxiety and depression.

I would have liked to find out more about her. It would have been an eye-opener if she'd kept a diary. And maybe it would have been helpful if she'd left a letter explaining how she felt. Maybe she could have been saved if she'd confided in someone and described how the addiction controlled her, why she found it so difficult to break it. Someone could have intervened if she'd opened up about her desire to take her own life, assuming the overdose that claimed her life was planned.

Everyone is aware of the damage caused by illegal drugs like cocaine, ice, or heroin, as the media constantly highlights these issues. But not many people know that a staggering number of ordinary men and women are in the throes of a terrible addiction to seemingly harmless pain tablets.

I began writing this diary in May 2015, hoping it would help me overcome my own addiction to codeine-based painkillers. This is an intimate account of what I've been through so far. My diary will give you an insight into the mind of an ordinary mum who became addicted without knowing it. Like other people in the same boat, I thought these tablets were harmless because you don't need a doctor's script to purchase them.

This diary relates my numerous attempts to overcome my addiction. Never giving up, I've remained hopeful in spite of countless relapses. I intend to write a follow-up to this diary that will describe my complete recovery and my new life without painkillers.

I want people to understand the seriousness of being hooked on these innocent-looking tablets. If you're like me and you're battling an addiction to over-the-counter medications or any other substance, please don't wait. Seek help immediately. Talk to a family member, a doctor, a counsellor, a trusted friend, or join a support group. It could save your life.

14 MAY 2015

"Could I please have a packet of ibuprofen with codeine tablets?" I don't know how many times I asked this question during the last few years.

And I don't know how many times the pharmacy assistant answered, "Are you on any other medication?" and "What are you taking this for?" This was followed by the usual advice of ingesting the tablets with food and only having a maximum of six per day. That made me laugh inside, in a sad sort of way, as I knew I would take more than six tablets of this well-known brand of painkiller.

I don't know exactly when it all started. If I look back into the past and try to pinpoint the first time I used codeine and felt good after taking it, it would probably take me back eight years. My youngest daughter, Angie, is almost ten years old at the writing of this book, and at the time, she would have been around two. I was working as an enrolled nurse doing night shift and had a stiff and painful neck. One of our aged care residents had recently died, and there was a packet of codeine-containing painkillers that was supposed to go back to the pharmacy, along with all other unused or expired medications, in a big plastic box. I knew this particular resident had been on those painkillers, as I had often given them to him as prescribed.

I opened the packet, extracted two of the oblong tablets, and swallowed them with some water. After some time, my pain subsided, and at the same time, I felt wonderful, happy, and energised. I walked around faster than usual, my head clear and focused, with enthusiasm and optimism about everything. I made sure all the work was done. I completed my paperwork in record time. I helped the carers with their duties, making beds and changing residents into incontinence pads.

An hour and a half later, I took another two painkiller tablets and felt even better. This effect lasted all night, and it made everything feel light and effortless during my shift. I believed I had found my panacea, the perfect remedy for all aches, fatigue, lack of motivation, and other difficulties I encountered. I loved these tablets, and they were to become my best friends over the next few years—whenever they were available.

To obtain these valuable tablets, I often stole them, which I had trouble admitting to myself. I didn't consider myself a thief; I was in denial. At first I thought nothing about taking a couple of tablets out of a resident's personal supplies, which were usually kept in a trolley to which I had access as an enrolled nurse. But over time, as I took more and more tablets, I felt increasingly uneasy about it.

Sometimes I would go as far as falsifying records, pretending I had given them to different residents who had these painkillers prescribed to them. I felt guilty and ashamed. I was scared to lose my registration if someone found out the truth. I could imagine my humiliation in front of my colleagues, my family, and all the people who would discover my dirty secret. I was terrified I would end up in jail.

Over time, it became more and more difficult to find tablets with codeine at work. I also felt increasingly guilty and ashamed about stealing them. I hated doing it, as I knew I was committing a crime, even when these tablets were meant to go back to the pharmacy to be destroyed. I decided to try over-the-counter painkillers with codeine in them. To begin, I took a popular brand that had paracetamol (acetaminophen) in it. But you can only take a maximum of eight a day, unless you want to put yourself at risk of severe liver damage and even death. The paracetamol is the damaging ingredient, although codeine has negative side effects of its own too.

I didn't want to die of liver failure, so I stuck to eight of these a day as much as possible, rarely getting up to twelve. I didn't experience many adverse side effects, except for the occasional nausea and dry mouth. But the overall effect of the drug wasn't as satisfying as the kick I would get out of the stronger brand with more codeine in it, which I obtained from my work place.

The over-the-counter medication was better than nothing. I could have easily obtained a prescription from any doctor if I'd made up a story about pain. I could have complained about chronic back pain, which a lot of nurses experience, especially in aged care. Aged care is heavy work that involves a lot of lifting. But I couldn't bring myself to lie to a doctor. There was a limit to what I was capable of, especially in the beginning. But as the addiction progressed, I did worse things than lying.

For around the next five years, I alternated between the stronger codeine tablets that I took at work, and the weaker brand that is sold over the counter in all pharmacies throughout Australia. There are so many pharmacies in Adelaide, it's easy to go to a different one every day to avoid suspicion. No one ever refused to sell me these tablets.

If I found a lot of unused tablets in the return pharmacy box, I would take some extra tablets to use later at home. At the time, I was convinced that this harmless drug was the best thing that had ever happened to me because it enabled me to work long hours without feeling fatigue and discouragement. I could stay focused for hours with this substance in my system. Sometimes I took them on my days off, just to get me through the day looking after my kids, shopping, cooking, cleaning, and putting up with all the stresses of ordinary life.

I also had to deal with the mood swings of my husband, Larry, who in my opinion drank too much beer. I had little patience, being exhausted most of the time, and my mind often reacted irrationally to what he said or did. I realise today that my attitude towards him was detrimental to our relationship. Larry works very hard as a glazier and usually comes home exhausted. Sometimes he just wants to be left alone and enjoy his beers after work, without having to put up with a nagging wife.

My addiction to codeine became an integral part of me. Even though I felt bad about it, I didn't think there was much wrong with it. It's a very common drug, and it's perfectly legal. You can go to any chemist in South Australia, and he or she will give you a packet of these tablets without fail, especially if you're reasonably dressed and come across as a normal citizen.

But I didn't want to take the risk of being caught stealing drugs from work anymore, so I tried another brand of codeine-based painkillers that could also be obtained without a prescription. It was a combination of ibuprofen and codeine, and it became my drug of choice. It was perfectly legal to purchase it, so I wasn't breaking the law. The codeine dosage is particularly high in this medication, but instead of containing paracetamol, it had ibuprofen, so I could take a lot of these tablets without having to worry about my liver—or so I believed.

I started off only taking six or eight a day. Soon I became hooked on them and took more than that. Sometimes I took twelve a day (all in one go, for the effect), and sometimes up to thirty tablets in two or three doses. I took handfuls of them, preferably on an empty stomach to maximise their effect, which is a kind of buzz similar to a high.

You're supposed to take this medication with food to avoid stomach ulcers, but I didn't care. In the end, I was regularly taking between twenty and thirty pills a day. I felt fatigued and had no drive when I didn't take these tablets, which made me take them more often just to alleviate these symptoms. Without this medication, I experienced withdrawal, but I didn't know it—or I didn't *want* to know it. I was in denial.

I was terrified of dying because I knew I was destroying my body. Ibuprofen can cause severe kidney damage. So while I was saving my liver, I was exposing my kidneys to abuse. I have also found out that ibuprofen causes liver damage, which I was also in denial about. Every drug you take is metabolised by the liver. If you take too much of any drug, your liver will suffer. I thought I was safe because I didn't drink any alcohol. That's how I fooled myself into believing I was superior to people who abused alcohol, when in fact I was probably doing worse.

The body is supposed to be the temple of the soul, and I was destroying it by taking these drugs. Like every addict, I tried to justify myself with irrational arguments, like telling myself I needed these tablets to get through my night shift. I couldn't admit that these arguments didn't make any sense if I was honest with myself. In the end, I had to use all the power of my objective reasoning to try to come to terms with this addiction. But I still couldn't let go of it. It had me in its grip, but I wanted to recover, no matter what it took.

Already, I've tried a lot of different strategies, including self-hypnosis, prayer, meditation, goal setting, and visualisation. I haven't done any counselling yet, but I think I will need to do it sooner or later if I truly want to get better. I'm ashamed about this secret that is slowly destroying me. I know it's a big mistake, but to this day, I can't bring myself to open up about it. I can't talk about it. Not to anyone—not even my husband. Not even a doctor. This is why I decided to keep this diary. It's my last-ditch attempt at getting clean. I don't like this word; it makes me feel like a druggie.

But the truth is that I am a codeine junkie. Or I was, as I don't want to define myself in that way anymore. Even if I say I'm an ex-codeine addict, I might go back to this drug. To me, these words are a self-fulfilling prophecy. If you say you're an ex-smoker, you're still using the word "smoker," and therefore it's a label you're giving to yourself. And you will live up to it and take up the habit again sooner or later. At least, this is what I believe. So I won't label myself. I'm just an ordinary person, a mum and a nurse, and I have a problem. I've become addicted to over-the-counter painkillers. It's a hurdle I need to overcome.

As of today I've lasted without this drug for over five days. It's been difficult to resist temptation. The first day wasn't too bad, as I still had a lot of codeine in my system. I felt tired, but I was functioning. It was Saturday, and the whole family went out to a restaurant to celebrate Flynn's birthday, my fourteen-year-old son. Everything was perfect; people were eating, laughing, and interacting lovingly and jokingly with each other like close family members do. When we're all together, no one suspects I have a problem.

On day two I still felt okay. I wasn't craving anything yet. I almost had a week off work ahead of me, and I wouldn't go back to my night shifts until the following weekend. I only work every second weekend in an attempt to curb my consumption of codeine. So far it hasn't worked. This time, I am determined things will be different. This diary is my salvation. Here I can talk about my problem, encourage myself, and record my progress. It is a good incentive to stay on track. I don't want to fall off the wagon because I will have to admit to it in these pages.

On day three, I began craving the substance my body has become accustomed to. I nearly went to the closest chemist to buy a packet of codeine painkillers. "I can just take six a day like it says on the packet," I tried to fool myself. Of course, I had never stuck with such resolutions. I would have consumed the whole packet of twenty or thirty tablets eventually, throwing fistfuls of tablets in my mouth, secretly in my car or in the bathroom, while no one was watching.

The empty packet would be disposed of with extreme care, wrapped in some papers or inside an empty package of cereal, before being dropped deep in the bin, preferably with another rubbish bag on top, to conceal any evidence of my problem to other people. I'm an expert at hiding things, and I never leave any evidence lying around. If I don't take all the tablets in a pack, I will flush the remaining ones down the drain, then dispose of the empty packet as I usually do.

Why do I destroy tablets I haven't used before throwing the packet in the bin? It's because I don't want to be tempted to get them out of the bin later on. It's just a crazy attempt at controlling my addiction. A rational person wouldn't understand, but anyone with an addiction knows what I'm talking about. The addictive mind is illogical and irrational. You end up not reasoning like a normal person.

From day four onwards, it has been a terrible roller coaster, mainly in my head. Physically, I don't have too many withdrawal symptoms, apart from a bit of anxiety, inability to focus, feeling lazy and unmotivated, restless legs when in bed, and night sweats (which I have anyway due to menopause, so I don't know if it's withdrawal or just my hormones). The conversation that goes on in my head always points me towards the next pharmacy. I don't know what has given me the strength to resist so far. There is one idea that I cling to and it's been helping me, and it goes like this:

"Whichever way you go, Abby, whether you decide to continue with your addiction or to quit it, you are going to suffer anyway. So it's better to suffer for a good cause and give up your addiction once and for all, replacing it with some good, wholesome habits. Being *healthy* means being whole, but if you pursue your addiction, you will cut a hole in your soul. This hole will get bigger and bigger until you die a miserable death."

There is this hole, this vacuum in my soul right now, and the addictive substance gives me an instant feeling of calm and love for myself and others. But as soon as the substance leaves my body, the void inside me becomes bigger, until I frantically, desperately, try to fill it up again. I try to cover it up, realising with terror that it has increased in size since last time.

The thought that no matter which way I go, *suffering* will be inevitable is a thought I cling to, as it makes sense to me. Yes, it will be hard, no matter which way I go, so I might as well choose the way that will keep me alive and in good health.

It's day six today. I have been able to cope to some degree, thanks to physical activity. I have been swimming every day since day two. This is the only way I can calm my body and my mind and do something about the restlessness I feel all the time. The endorphins must help. But even as I swim laps in the pool, I have to encourage myself because I tend to get panic attacks.

To stop the fear rising in my chest, I focus on my breathing and put my thoughts on something happening around me, like the music coming out of the speakers. I watch other people swimming or walking in the pool. There are no children doing swimming lessons this week. The schools are doing some testing ordered by the government. I was lucky to have a lane to myself almost every day. This is how quiet it was, and I felt grateful for it. I didn't want to get stressed by other swimmers crowding me.

Today is the first day I'm writing in this journal, and already it gives me a lot of relief. I want to keep doing it and will be back tonight before going off to sleep. This is the best thing that's happened to me—deciding to write down my struggle to overcome this addiction.

Tonight I feel very tired. I tend to get rapidly exhausted without my fix. I also had a hunger attack and ate anything I could put my hands on: cheese, biscuits, cake … I'm going to put on weight, but I don't care. It's not important after all—and I'd rather be fat and increase my chances of survival. It's only 9:30 p.m. and I can't keep myself from yawning. Normally I'm a night owl, and codeine keeps me awake, but without my tablets, I have no energy. But I have been able to resist temptation when I was just about to drive to the chemist several times today. I managed to do this only because I was thinking about my diary and how disappointed I would be in myself if I had to start it all over. No matter what happens, I won't give up, and I *will* be successful.

I have to get out of my head that codeine is something desirable. When I used to smoke, many years ago, I found cigarettes enjoyable. Now I find them quite disgusting. I want the same to happen for codeine. I love it now, but eventually, I will hate it. I won't even want it anymore. I know this will happen for me. For the time being, I will be persistent and psyche myself up as much as possible. I have to do it all the time, or I will fall off the wagon. I have to keep in mind my ultimate goal: to stay clean and lead a healthy and productive life. I want to live to be a hundred years old.

15 MAY 2015

TODAY IS DAY SEVEN WITHOUT any painkillers. Hooray, I haven't had anything with codeine in it for seven days—the longest I've lasted in years. Usually I can go for two or three days, until my brain tells me that just a few tablets will make me feel better. Until my brain makes me believe I can control my intake and stick to the recommended six tablets a day. What a joke, but at those times, I believe it. That's how my addicted mind plays games with me, convincing me it's okay to have maybe eight or ten or even twelve tablets, all in one go for the effect, the momentary buzz they give me. And then soon it's back to twenty-four or thirty tablets a day.

I felt awful this morning, waking up with a pounding headache, blurred vision, my back aching, and not wanting to get out of bed, even though I couldn't sleep. I was thinking, *What is there to live for? Another day of agony and craving something I can't have.* I went back to bed after getting Angie ready for school. I felt bad because I was short-tempered and impatient with her. This is how I feel at the moment. I have no inner resources to deal with daily stresses. This is why I formed this habit in the first place.

I couldn't cope with day-to-day life anymore. I was trying to raise five children on my own, while my husband Larry did little to help me and often put me down as well. I must admit I was hypersensitive to his criticism, and I tended to interpret the things he said in a hurtful way.

Larry stopped drinking beer about two years ago. He did it quietly on his own, without advertising it. This is how I want to stop my habit too, which he knows nothing about. It's hard to drink secretly, because the smell gives you away. But it's easy to abuse over-the-counter painkillers with codeine. They don't smell, and they don't change your behaviour. You just become more relaxed and more able to cope with everything. You can work, study, do the housework, and do everything you want, but do it *better*. You just perform better with them. This is why I love these tablets so much. Some people say codeine makes them drowsy, but I have never noticed this negative side-effect. To me, codeine is an upper, and it helps me stay awake and function when I'm exhausted or have to work night shifts.

After I got up this morning, I had a coffee, which made me jittery. I couldn't eat anything, so I drank a sweet milk drink, and then I drove to the chemist. But thanks to God I didn't buy any codeine painkillers. I only wanted something to get rid of my headache, so I asked for an anti-inflammatory, but nothing with codeine in it. The pills I got did the job, and my headache vanished. I felt much better, even though restless and anxious and dashing to the toilet every twenty minutes with the worst diarrhea. I took two lots of anti-diarrhoea tablets that I had purchased previously. Every forum on detox tells you to have these ready if you want to come off opiates. I read so many of these forum entries hoping to figure out how to deal with this, but I didn't find too many answers. *Time* seems to be the only cure for this addiction.

Day seven, and I feel slightly better compared to day four or five, but still not back to normal, whatever that is, as I haven't felt "normal" for years. I remember giving up cigarettes a long time ago, and even though I had been puffing for at least fifteen years, I felt good after the first three days. I didn't experience any withdrawal symptoms or any desire to go back to smoking. The same happened when I gave up drinking alcohol five years ago. It was so easy compared to this.

To anyone who is taking more than the prescribed amount of codeine-based painkillers, please listen to me and stop *now* before it is too late. You don't realise how much damage you're doing to yourself with this seemingly innocent habit. It will destroy you and might even kill you in the end. Don't think you'll ever be able to control it: That's an illusion, your ego convincing you that you don't have a problem and are able to quit any time. I understand how alcoholics and drug addicts feel now, because I am no better than them. I am one of them, but I will beat this no matter what. This is not what I desire for myself, my life. I had other plans, and dying of a painkiller overdose wasn't one of them.

I am forty-nine years old, almost fifty. My birthday is coming up, and I don't want to spend the next decade like I spent this one. I have basically wasted my life, thrown away the precious present my creator gave me. If I could turn back the clock and start all over, I would never touch anything with codeine in it. This is the devil in disguise, telling you how harmless he is, when in reality he wants to have total power over you and destroy you so he can claim your soul.

I have five beautiful children ranging from the ages of nine to twenty-one. They are wonderful and well adjusted, in spite of all the ups and downs we've been through as a family. I have always shown them love and understanding, even in times of great difficulty. They are innocent and don't know anything about this. I don't want them to find out. They have so much respect and admiration for me, and I don't want this image to be tarnished. It's not so much my ego that stops me from telling them the truth. Why should they know? It would only worry them. I can beat this on my own, without making a drama out of it. All I need to do is stick with my resolution once and for all.

Today is a very important day because I go back to work tonight. This will be a test to see if I can stay clean at work. I have to do it—no matter what. If my resolve weakens and I take anything with codeine in it, I will be back to square one, and all this hard work will be for nothing. Please, God, give me the strength to do this, so I can be there for my family and live my life in peace, without this horrible addiction.

Yesterday I read something about "codeine water extraction" on a forum. It's a simple method to extract the codeine from your tablets and avoid the ibuprofen and paracetamol that do so much damage to your body, much more than codeine does (which isn't harmless, of course). I even watched an online video about it. It had over 350,000 views. Why had I never thought about it before, instead of risking my liver and kidneys? But how would I do it anyway? I'm always being watched in this house. My children are here most of the time. I only have time to myself when they're at school or at university (my oldest son Daniel is studying architecture).

And what do you do when you spontaneously want to pop a few tablets to instantly feel better? What do you do when you're at work and need to stay awake? It means you have to plan your addiction a lot better and *prepare* yourself. Have your drug ready for when you need it. It takes a bit of time management. I was very tempted to give it a go, but I won't. It's too late for that now.

What helped me so far over the last seven days: a lot of exercise (I went swimming every day, except for today) as it alleviates symptoms of restless legs and anxiety, although I had a panic attack while I was in the pool last time, and it wasn't pleasant. I managed to talk myself out of it and continued swimming in spite of it.

I took herbal remedies to help me sleep, even though they were not very effective, but the placebo effect helped a little. If I had a headache, I took two paracetamol tablets. I drank a lot of water. I took it easy and didn't worry too much about cleaning the house. I didn't cook much either, and it was take-away dinners on most nights, which the kids don't complain about anyway, and Larry prefers to cook his own food. Whenever I began thinking about codeine, I tried to take my mind off it and find something leisurely to do, like watch a TV show or go to my piano. One positive thing so far: my piano playing has improved.

I am thinking about ways to replace my addiction with something better. I believe that to let go of a bad habit, you need to replace it with a good one. One day, I want to give talks about motivation and willpower. I want to learn yoga and incorporate it in my daily routine. I want to meditate too, as it is such a calming thing to do. I think yoga would be a good idea. I've always wanted to do yoga since I was thirteen years old. I had a book about it, which I used to take with me everywhere. I would look at the illustrations of the different poses and techniques, attempting them occasionally and promising myself that one day, I would make them an essential part of my daily routine. Now it's time to do it, and I will start taking classes after completing my night shifts.

23 MAY 2015

Unfortunately, today I'm back to square one. I broke my promise. I went back to taking codeine painkillers. I couldn't cope with what I had to do. I couldn't face my life and obligations without these tablets. But now I am full of regrets, discouraged, and depressed. I feel like a failure. I am not good at this. A huge part of the problem is *work*. Before I went back to my shifts, I panicked, just thinking about the work load and the stress. I was picturing the interminably long hours I would be working, dead tired, while other "normal" people would be comfortably asleep in their beds.

My resolve became weaker, until I decided to do the "cold water extraction." I had watched this guy doing it and explaining it on the video, and it looked as easy as child's play. At least it would spare my liver, but on the whole it was rather disappointing. To make sure it would be effective, I used heaps of tablets, but even though I followed all the instructions, I found that it didn't work as well as I had expected. The feeling of euphoria just wasn't there, the high I normally get out of these tablets. Even though I persevered with the process all weekend, I didn't get out of it what I hoped for. Maybe it would be better if I placed my hope in other things, like getting better at yoga and meditation.

Then on Sunday morning, as I was ready to go back home from night shift, someone told me my car had been broken into. My handbag, which I had hidden under the seat, had been stolen, along with my wallet and all my cards in it. There wasn't any cash in the wallet, but I felt terrible. I felt violated and couldn't understand why someone would smash a car just to access a wallet. The door was all bent and damaged, and the repairs will be expensive, as it will require panel beating. I was devastated.

I overreacted and used the break-in as an excuse to indulge into more over-the-counter tablets. There was now a good excuse to consume heaps of tablets and feel sorry for myself. I was just imagining how much all this would cost me and the hassles of putting everything right. I wasn't thinking straight, not putting things into perspective. My addicted mind blew everything out of proportion.

My wonderful son Daniel offered to pay for a new window right away. He asked me how much it would cost, and I roughly estimated it would be $450. He drove to the cash machine and got out $500. I was very touched, as he really looks out for me and cares about me. He hates seeing me unhappy or stressed out. I feel bad that I abuse myself. I should be looking after myself and making sure nothing happens to me. I could die from this addiction by damaging my liver or my kidneys.

My husband Larry was quite concerned and helpful too, except that he didn't offer to pay for anything. We have separate accounts, this being a second marriage for both of us. It was his wish to do it that way, not mine. He protects himself because he earns a lot more money than I do.

Sometimes I feel that Larry doesn't care about me, so I don't tell him much about myself. This is why I prefer to keep my addiction a secret. He wouldn't understand, and I'm afraid he wouldn't have any sympathy for me. I feel like crying now. I feel lonely and desperate, and I make it look like he is a bad person, but he is not. I am being unfair. He has helped me, even though it doesn't feel like it, especially at times when I like to feel sorry for myself. I must admit that I tend to remember the bad things and forget the good ones.

He accepted me with four children from a previous marriage. It didn't happen without difficulty—but he did it anyway, and he has treated them well. Not like his own children—but at least he hasn't been unfair towards them. He could have turned away from me when he met me over a decade ago, but he didn't. Our relationship was rocky for a long time, but it has improved over the last couple of years. We don't argue anymore. We used to have terrible arguments, and it was partly my fault, because I had an anger problem. This contributed to my turning to over-the-counter drugs. I wanted something to calm me down.

I also needed something to help me cope with stress. Being responsible for four children, then five, as we had Angie together (she is our only common child), was a lot of work. I accused him of being unsupportive. I left him once, but then I went back because I loved him. From then on, he tried to please me more and was more caring and patient. He became a better person, but I don't know if I can say the same about myself. He has changed for the better, but I don't think I've improved much.

My daughter Fiona is twenty years old and doing an arts degree. She moved out of our home about two years ago to live with her boyfriend, Rick. Rick has his own landscape and gardening business, and he is very successful. I think Fiona became fed up with me. She had to support me emotionally for many years, especially during times when my marriage was rocky, and Larry and I used to argue a lot.

Fiona would reassure the younger children. She often did the cooking and cleaning for me when I was too exhausted or too upset to do the chores. I still feel bad for her, as it's not fair on a child having to do these things. I would spoil her in other ways, buy her nice clothes and give her money for household chores, but it didn't make up for the carefree childhood she missed out on. She is more at peace now, since she's moved in with Ricky, but it doesn't erase my guilt. I feel bad for forcing her to grow up too fast because of my problems.

When she was living at home, I bought a horse for Fiona, Snowdrop, a beautiful white mare, proud and wild like a unicorn. I worked a lot of night shifts for that horse, but I don't regret doing it for my daughter. She shared Snowdrop with her sister Georgia. They would take turns riding it. I encouraged their passion for horse riding, no matter how much I had to sweat for it. I nearly worked myself into the ground paying for their expensive hobby, but it made me feel good, maybe because it compensated for the lack of good parenting during their formative years. I loved Snowdrop. I didn't mind paying for her stabling fees and all the other costs, like the farrier, the veterinarian, the equine dental veterinarian, pony club fees, and private horse riding fees. I took codeine painkillers at work to keep me going so I could pay for everything. Georgia is now eighteen and will finish school this year. She wants to study psychology.

Flynn is almost fifteen and very much like his brother Daniel. They both love sports, especially tennis and beach volleyball. Flynn is a good boy. I never had any problems with him. He goes to a private school because I don't want him to be subjected to negative influences or get bullied in the public system. (In Australia public schools are *really* public, not like in England.) If you live in a low socio-economic area like we do, you can expect a lot of kids from dysfunctional backgrounds. The result: bad language, bad attitude, violence, and drugs are rampant, as well as wagging (cutting school).

School fees for Flynn mean another $10,000 a year for me. My ex-husband Brett, who is the father of the four older children Daniel, Fiona, Georgia, and Flynn, pays some maintenance, but not enough, in my opinion. He is a bricklayer and doesn't always get regular work. The maintenance he pays just covers Brendan's school fees, but little else. I have to pay for all the food, clothing, Internet, school uniforms, school supplies which includes a compulsory laptop, extra-curricular activities, and so on. The list is never-ending. I don't know how I managed all these years.

Larry gives me a weekly allowance for Angie, but it is only a relatively small amount, and it doesn't even cover half of her costs. She does gymnastics, piano, and horse-riding at a riding school. She would like to have her own pony too, but I don't think I'll be able to afford a horse again. My objective is to overcome my addiction. I need to put myself first if I want to succeed.

Fiona and Georgia enjoyed Snowdrop for many years. We had to give her away in the end because Fiona became too busy during her last year at school, and I found it increasingly difficult to pay for her stable fees because I didn't get as many shifts with the agency that employed me. It has become more difficult for enrolled nurses to get work because a lot of places prefer to employ registered nurses. We found a wonderful new owner for Snowdrop, one of Fiona's horse riding friends. My daughters miss Snowdrop to this day, and so do I. But it is better for my bank account not to have her. I would like to be able to realise the dream of owning a pony or a horse for Angie. I would like her to enjoy the unique bond with this magnificent animal. Maybe one day it will happen, once she is a more advanced and confident rider.

But first I have to focus *totally* on myself, on giving up my addiction once and for all. This has to be my priority, before anything else. I don't know *how* I will do it, but I know I will. This is my last chance. I know I said this last time, and I say it every time, but this time I have *no excuses*. I have to do it, no matter what, and I can only do it *one day at a time*, and hope for the best. I need to replace this negative habit with something positive: yoga and meditation. I know I suffer from *stress*, and have done so for a long time. This is probably the reason why I turned to over-the-counter painkillers—to kill the pain caused by stress.

I felt so tired this afternoon that I had to go to sleep for a couple of hours. Georgia kept pestering me for money. She wanted me to drive her to a party and pick her up afterwards. She was nasty to me, and when I went back to my bedroom I was sobbing. Larry was there. He was really nice to me and gave me a hug. Then in the evening, he offered to drive her. The way Georgia treats me sometimes is depressing, and I'm not sure what to do about it. Or maybe it's just *me*. Am I hypersensitive, due to withdrawal? When you're on painkillers you don't feel anything, but today it's only day one, and I'm already raw and things seem to get under my skin easily and affect me quickly.

Maybe I am depressed and need antidepressants. Maybe that's why I turned to over-the-counter analgesics in the first place. Or am I depressed because I suffer from withdrawal? I would like to be able to stay away from these drugs for two weeks so I can find out for sure. If I am depressed, then I can do something about it. Sometimes I feel like there is something wrong with my brain. After what I've been through in the last ten or eleven years, maybe it's a normal reaction, some kind of post traumatic stress disorder. My divorce from Brett was difficult, and the years after that were a constant struggle. And today everything seems to be too much for me, and I can't cope with anything. Even work is too much for me. I can't work like a normal person, forty hours a week, from nine to five.

I was looking for some helpful ideas on how to break an addiction. An interesting concept is to refuse to acknowledge failure. "Eliminate failure from your vocabulary." People who succeed are those who have unrealistic expectations.

They don't go by their own track record. For instance, J. K. Rowling got twelve refusals from publishers before she found one who agreed to publish Harry Potter. Edison did thousands of experiments that failed before he developed the light bulb. There are countless examples of people who didn't give up. Even though they failed hundreds of times, they believed they could still succeed.

Already, I've tried numerous times to come off this terrible substance without success, but I refuse to give up. I'm here to continue and to win this battle, in spite of my past record. There is no failure. Each time an attempt is fruitless, I can learn from it. And each time, that little bit of extra knowledge might be enough to propel me forward a little further. I know that *this* time, I can do it, even though I've failed hundreds of times before. But I can't subscribe to the idea of powerlessness, as suggested in some recovery programmes. I want to take my power into my own hands and use it in my struggle to beat this demon. I won't give my power away. And I can't keep giving it away to an over-the-counter drug.

To me, powerlessness feels like giving up. It implies I don't have the resources within myself to come to terms with this. Codeine seems to give me a sense of relief from a reality that I can't handle, but that doesn't mean I can't live without these tablets. Other things give people a sense of relief, like food, sex, or gambling. It doesn't mean that everyone is out of control just because they gain a sense of satisfaction from something. As humans, we do have the ability to control ourselves and master our impulses. I believe in this, and I can't embrace the powerlessness ideology. Maybe it suits other people, but it's not for me. I need to find something for myself that works, that sustains me, but not the idea that I am powerless. Good mental health means feeling empowered, after all, not feeling defeated. I want to believe that *I can do it,* that I have the power within myself to overcome this.

25 MAY 2015

DAY THREE OF THIS SECOND attempt, and I feel that I have to go through the same process all over again. I nearly went seven days without codeine painkillers before I started again. I took over-the-counter codeine-based painkillers for a week before deciding to stop again. Now I have to pay the price for it. I feel weak and unmotivated, like I don't want to do anything. This morning, I could barely drag myself out of bed to get Angie ready for school. I went to bed at 8:30 p.m. the night before, and it was 7:15 a.m. when my alarm went off. I felt like I hadn't slept at all and badly wanted to stay within the safety of my sheets and blankets.

Is this depression? Maybe I should go to the doctor and get a prescription for an antidepressant. I have tried taking antidepressants several times in the past, but they didn't help much, just made me feel tired. It also affected my sleep, and I felt worse after a few days, which made me stop the medicine. But maybe I should have persisted and taken it for at least two or three weeks. That's when the changes are supposed to happen, as the drug needs to build up in your system. I don't know if it's true and if it really works, as I've never had enough patience to wait, and instead I preferred to go back to my old friend codeine. It seems to be so much more effective and immediately takes away my lack of drive. When I take codeine, I can do things for hours, even things I don't feel like doing. I become a robot, a machine, until the drug wears off and I feel worse than I did before.

Right now, I'm so down that I don't know how I even manage to write this. I really have to force myself. This is my only hope or I would be at the chemist right now, asking for a packet of codeine painkillers and swallowing a handful of tablets within minutes of buying it. Then I would feel better for a while, even though the feeling would be mixed with a sense of guilt and despair. But I would fool myself and make myself believe that this is the last time I'm doing it, and tomorrow I'll give up this nasty habit once and for all. There is always tomorrow, and there is always hope. That's the beauty of life. You can always decide to start something tomorrow—instead of doing it right now. Tomorrow is a chance that can turn into the biggest excuse. Binge eaters, alcoholics, drug takers, and smokers probably all go through the same thing and use the same reasoning. They convince themselves that tomorrow they will finally be able to quit their addiction.

The person who has a problem with food will say, "Let's have a binge today. Today I can eat anything I want, and tomorrow I'll go on a diet." How many times have people made these resolutions? They do it over and over, only to become weak again after a few days and give in to the urge to overeat or abuse their drug of choice.

I want to find a reliable strategy to overcome my addiction. So far I haven't been very successful. And it's so easy to lose your motivation when you don't have your drug of choice in your system. It's easy to decide to be clean when you've just swallowed a packet of tablets. I take this drug because it makes me feel better. I become energised, and I'm able to cope with the demands of my life. I can deal better with my children, my job, my husband, my chronic lack of money, and so on. It's a constant uphill battle, and there seems to be no way out of it.

We are a lower middle class family—or should I say "upper working class?" My income as a part-time enrolled nurse is low, not enough to survive on unless you're an extremely disciplined person who never wastes a dollar. This is how disciplined I am in some areas, as I have managed to live without taking up a credit or loan, and yet I can't control myself in other areas, especially with my addiction. Sometimes I feel that the cards are stacked against me, that this substance is controlling me, because I haven't been able to control my life, my emotions, my fears.

Even though I don't have much money and Larry doesn't support me enough financially (in my opinion), I manage to make ends meet. I have high aspirations for my children and will spend what is necessary for them to get a good education. I could work more hours as an enrolled nurse, but I get stressed about it and I can't find any satisfaction in my job anymore. I have been feeling burnt out for a long time, and I have lost my passion for nursing over the years. It is a sad thing, but now I just do it for the money.

I still do a good job, and I show compassion to the elderly. I would never abuse or neglect sick and frail people. But I have come to depend on painkillers to enable me to do my job, to be able to function. So if I work more, it means more over-the-counter painkillers just to dull myself so I can do my work on auto-pilot. It seems this is the only way for me to cope. I tried doing it differently, but it didn't last very long. I would like to write books and eventually be able to quit nursing altogether. I would like to write something about my own experience with addiction and how I overcame it.

I don't know where this diary will lead me, but it is my only chance. I'm clinging to it like a drowning person to a piece of wood from a shipwreck. But I have no reason to be unhappy or dissatisfied with my life. This weekend, we had a lovely family reunion with all my children at a beautiful café in the hills. We spent three hours there, because we had to wait a long time for our meals. We used this time to talk and bond as a family. Larry was there too, and he was happy being with us, and in the end he split the bill with me. I paid for all my children, even though I can't really afford it on my small nurse's income. I do it because I love my kids, I love Fiona's boyfriend Rick, and I love to see us all together and getting along well, Daniel, Georgia, Flynn, and Angie. I love them to bits, and I am doing this for them because I want to be there for them in the future.

I could die if I continue taking codeine painkiller tablets. This is what I need to remind myself. Positive motivation doesn't always work, so I have to frighten myself into doing this. I have tried so many times and I only have a few days left until I turn fifty. I don't want to die an early death when I have everything going for me. I'm not saying that my life is perfect, but whose life is?

I am quite healthy if you take away my addiction. I can't remember the last time I was sick. I have a good enough husband, even though we've been through a lot of ups and downs, but we are still together, and we love each other in spite of everything. I have five wonderful, well-adjusted children, and I am proud of them. So what else can I ask for? Money is not exactly flowing into my life yet, but who knows? With a positive attitude everything is possible, and I could be prosperous a few years down the road. Everything starts with *gratitude,* and this is what I need to focus on. A gratitude mindset will stop me from feeling sorry for myself and falling into the trap of using drugs. This is a new awareness, and maybe this kind of awareness is the key to permanent change. It's a sort of discipline to have on a daily basis, like eating the right food and exercising regularly.

What else can I think of that might help me? Maybe another strategy is to forget about the drugs, to put them out of my mind and be aware when the thought of them enters my mind. And as soon as the thought is there, delete it right away.

26 MAY 2015

I HAVE BEEN TRYING MY latest strategy of putting this cunning substance out of my mind, but it's hard to stop yourself from thinking something, especially when your body and mind are crying out for it. I can't remember when I last felt so bad in my own body. I'm restless and edgy, unable to enjoy anything. The only thing that keeps me going is this diary. I know that if I fail, I will have to give it up. I won't make another start again. I have to keep moving forward, no matter what, and accept a life without my chemical crutch.

Swimming one kilometre helped this morning. I felt slightly better afterwards and wasn't so tense. I feel scared, but I don't know exactly what I'm frightened of. Maybe not being able to make it! If I don't, I will die, I know this for sure. This habit will slowly but surely kill me, and I can't do this to my family, especially to my children. The only thing that keeps me going is my love for them, knowing they need me. They have always been very close to me. When they have problems, they come to me; they can trust me. I have never rejected them or treated them with indifference. I have always made time for them, even when I was busy working or doing other things.

My children will always come first in my life. I don't care as much about Larry. I find that he doesn't show me much affection, even though I know he loves me in his own way. I often yearn for something better, more intense—a love that is reciprocated, not one-sided. He doesn't show me he loves me the same way I love him. Larry used to put me down a lot, but fortunately he doesn't do this anymore.

It's important that I remind myself why I am doing this. It will keep me going. My children are my life, and I am doing this for them. Sometimes I feel like I am in a living hell inside, but on the outside, I look perfectly normal. I act normally. My behaviour is no different from what it usually is. I have perfected the art of self-control, or I am able to conceal what I feel. I hide my feelings so I don't hurt others.

27 MAY 2015

TODAY IS DAY FIVE, AND I've nearly reached the end of my tether. I can't stand it anymore! What does it feel like to be in my shoes? It feels like you've got absolutely no drive, no motivation. I just don't want to do anything. I have to force myself to do every single thing that needs to be done, like preparing Angie's and Flynn's dinner and lunchboxes, taking washing from the line, putting new sheets on the beds, which I hadn't done for a couple of months. Every single action I perform requires mountains of willpower, but I haven't given in to the urge to buy a packet of painkillers. I came close to it a few times. The temptation was strong, but then I thought about this diary, and I felt guilty. I don't want to start all over again. I mean, how many times am I going to do this?

It only takes twenty-one days to form new habits. This is the minimum time frame. According to Google, the "twenty-one days to form a habit" idea comes from a self-help book by a cosmetic surgeon, Dr. Maxwell Maltz. The book is called *Psycho Cybernetics*. I am unsure how he proved it, as I haven't read his book yet, but I'm sure it must take longer to change your habits. But after three weeks, I would know I'm on the right track, and I'm sure I would be able to continue without failing all the time. I'd be able to notice the changes in my body and my mind.

I can do this for three weeks, I'm repeating to myself. Only three weeks—it's not the end of the world. In the meantime, I don't seem to be able to motivate myself to do anything. I used to take this drug to give me courage, up-and-go, and stamina. With codeine in my system, I could do things for hours at a time, like housework or writing or playing the piano. I would never feel tired or fed up. Now that's all I feel: an immense tiredness. I am worn out even before I begin a task. Just thinking about it makes me weary. Is this depression? Maybe it's just part of the withdrawal process, feeling really bad. No aches and pains though, and no diarrhea. Maybe I'm already past that stage. Now it's the psychological addiction I have to deal with, and that's the tricky part, the worst part.

A voice in my head keeps telling me that it's not worth doing, that I should give up now, that I should buy a packet of codeine painkillers and just take a couple of tablets. A couple of tablets won't do me any harm. I can use this drug like a normal person does. I listen to this voice for a while. Then I decide to push it away, because I know it is lying to me. It's the addiction talking. Over and over, it comes back with the same old argument that I have this substance under control and that it isn't a problem to use it in moderation.

But addicts can't do things in moderation, or they wouldn't be addicts. They would be normal people and wouldn't have a problem. They wouldn't go out at 8 p.m. to get a packet of codeine-based over-the-counter analgesics just to ease the pain of being alive and having to put up with all the stress, repetition, and dreariness that comes with it. From the time I get up in the morning, life to me seems to be an endless cycle of mundane chores. Even getting out of bed is a chore. I dread that moment and delay it as much as possible, even if I just lie in bed and do nothing. As soon as I put my foot on the ground, I feel like I'm on an endless treadmill until I can go to sleep again. Sleep is the only redeeming quality I can find in life.

Life is not really worth living. I know it sound awfully negative, but I'm just being honest here, and this is how I feel inside. Why pretend otherwise? I will never tell my family about this, because they think I am one of the most positive people ever, always full of humour and energy.

28 MAY 2015

TODAY I REACHED DAY SIX. I can't give up now, not after nearly a week! It would be too stupid. This is why I keep writing in this diary, because I can feel myself falling off the wagon and losing my resolve. I have to straighten myself up and keep walking along this path, no matter how difficult and treacherous it looks. I wouldn't wish this on my worst enemy, the mental torment and the absolute longing for a substance that you know will make you feel better—a substance you also know might kill you in the end.

What did I do today to help overcome my craving for this substance? I didn't try to psyche myself up because I knew it wouldn't work, not while going through withdrawal. I ate a lot, salads, bread, cheese, biscuits, and cakes. It filled the void, even though it means doing a marathon swim tomorrow to burn it all off. I don't care; all I want is stay on track without going backwards.

I have trouble sleeping at night. I wake up every hour or every two hours, and I am exhausted in the morning. On top of that, Larry is a night owl who goes to bed late, and he woke me up after midnight, just when I was beginning to doze off. He doesn't do it on purpose. He's just noisy when he brushes his teeth and gets ready for bed. He turns on the lights and rummages in his bedside drawer.

Now all I need to do is to become clean. Codeine has a reputation of being as bad as heroin, and I don't doubt it. It seems to be just as difficult to come off this drug. I have given up a few things in my life, like cigarettes, alcohol, sleeping tablets (benzodiazepines), overeating (I used to be a binge eater), and nail biting. This one is the most difficult habit to give up. I don't know what it does to my brain, but it must interfere with a lot of processes. I feel tense and unfocused, without energy, and without any inclination to do anything productive. The only reason I'm writing this is that if I don't, I will drive to the closest chemist and get my dose. I will buy a packet of twenty-four codeine painkiller tablets and swallow them all at once.

I want to take my mind off this drug as much as possible, even though it doesn't always work. My mind strays and goes back there all the time. It's like a wild horse, and I need to grab the reins and lead it back—back to where? I'm not quite sure. Back to *normality* I guess, to inner peace without drugs. Back to being a healthy person, not an addict. I wish I could restore my whole system to an earlier point, just like a computer. I need to go back in time, at least ten years ago. I was quite "normal" back then. I just used to drink a bit too much alcohol at times, like on weekends, but apart from that I was quite healthy.

All I need to do is go back to the person I was before I discovered over-the-counter codeine painkillers and what they could do to help me cope with life. I can blame my addiction on a lot of things, like my divorce from Brett, then the rocky relationship I had with Larry. I could blame it on my stressful job as an enrolled nurse in aged care, doing night shifts to support my children from my first marriage. My ex-husband Brett is a bricklayer on a fairly low income, and the maintenance he pays me monthly is just enough to cover school fees for Flynn. Nothing else, no additional costs like uniforms, laptops, books, or lunches. Flynn's laptop recently broke, and I have to find $500 to buy him a new one.

I always worry about money. No one suspects I have a money problem because I never talk about it. I don't know how I keep things running the way they are, supporting my kids and buying all their food and clothes. Sometimes I am so desperate that I shoplift items I can't afford. It's not something I'm proud of, but I admit to it because I don't want to be a liar. This is a truthful account of my struggle. I can't hide anything from these pages, whether I'm ashamed of it or not. Guilt and shame have been part of my life for so long that they seem normal to me. A learnt response maybe, but a well-integrated one, so much part of my person that sometimes I go to the other extreme of not caring at all about what I do.

It's like an internal rebellion going on. Maybe I'm still a teenager at war with an adult world I have trouble accepting. All the rules and principles, and the fact that I have to work to make money, this is what I resent the most. I don't reject work out of laziness. I just want to do something I'm passionate about, not go to work like a well-oiled machine, a robot performing certain tasks mechanically, without any heart and soul. Codeine helps me function like that. It helps me do any job, any task I would normally recoil from. This is why it has become such an important part of my life. Without it, I feel that I can't be a productive human being.

They say life is an illusion, and this is just a big dream. I would call it a nightmare at the moment, and I hope I will wake up from it soon. If this is a "dream," why is everything so hard? Why does it take so much inner drive to accomplish anything? I feel like I am in one of those nightmares where you try to run away from something, but your legs won't move, or they only move slowly. When I take codeine, I have this bouncy energy I can't find otherwise. It gives me the feeling of being able to tackle anything, but it makes me tired and depressed the next day, like a hangover.

6 JUNE 2015

Last time I attempted to give up codeine painkillers, I reached day seven before I relapsed severely. It was Friday and I had to go back to work, but I was dreading it. In my distorted mind, I thought I would only be able to get through the night if I took a few codeine painkiller tablets, so after deliberating unsuccessfully within myself, I got into my car and drove to the closest chemist. They were just about to close for the day, and I quickly bought a pack of twenty-four tablets, using a migraine headache as a pretext. From then on, it was a downward spiral all the long weekend. Monday was a public holiday and my last night duty at the nursing home.

I looked in the drug cupboard and pinched two packets of strong codeine-containing painkillers, which I knew these residents didn't need anymore; they never showed any signs of pain or discomfort. I took handfuls of these tablets during the next few nights that I was on duty, and the codeine kept me going. I joked around with the carers and managed to finish all my paperwork. I was very efficient and felt on top of the world. No negative side effects, and I wasn't hungry, which suited me fine as I'm always trying to lose weight. Not that I really need to lose much, but I've had an obsession with weight since I was a teenager.

My mother had brainwashed me into thinking I was too fat. She didn't know and maybe didn't *want* to know that I felt lonely and depressed. I had trouble making friends in high school, and I longed for love in my life. I grew up with dysfunctional parents: a controlling, obsessive, and critical mother and a volatile, alcoholic father. I can't remember receiving much love at home, only a lot of criticism.

My mother is a "mean" person, according to my younger sister Sally-Ann. She didn't do much to give me a healthy self-esteem. But today I don't need to be resentful towards her anymore. She went through a lot in her own life, being a child during the Second World War. Today I feel sorry for her, especially since she's been diagnosed with breast cancer. I only found out about her diagnosis less than a week ago; my other sister Jill called me to tell me the bad news. I could blame my mother for my wobbly self-esteem, but I have made choices in my life that I could have avoided. I didn't respect myself, and in my younger days, I was starving for love but went about it the wrong way. Maybe I was a love addict. Today I'm a codeine addict.

I finished my nights on Tuesday morning, the second of June, my fiftieth birthday. I wasn't excited about it, and if I had known what was about to happen, I would have looked even less forward to it. I had emptied both packets of codeine painkillers I had found at work, and I also came across a packet of tramadol that was due to go back because the doctor had ceased the medication. I took it and immediately swallowed some capsules, six at a time, at 50 mg strength each. I usually don't take this drug, as I've had some bad experiences with it in the past. First it makes me feel euphoric and full of energy. It's a weird feeling, like I'm in love with the whole world and want to hug everyone. At the same time I can jump around and do all these physical things like touching my toes or doing a back bend. I don't feel anything, just pure energy. I know it sounds weird, but it's as if I'd taken amphetamines, even though I've never taken any, but I imagine that's what it would feel like.

To make myself feel better, I remind myself that I don't drink any alcohol and haven't done so for a number of years, I think seven years altogether. It just happened out of the blue. One day I decided to stop drinking and never touched a drop of alcohol again. I was ready to give it up and live my life without it. If I still drank today, I would probably turn into an alcoholic, and I wouldn't be able to hide it as easily as my addiction to painkillers. You can always tell when someone's been drinking by the smell on their breath and on their body. Not with codeine painkillers. They don't smell, and your behaviour doesn't get affected. It's only on the inside that it changes you. You feel this instant calm and warm sensation in your body. You feel so good, and when you stop taking it, it's all gone and everything becomes raw and edgy. The softness, the ease is gone, and things become awkward and difficult. I lose my patience and start crying for the smallest thing. When I don't have codeine in my system, I'm like an appliance without electricity.

So I had all this tramadol in my system on the morning of my birthday. It's a much stronger painkiller than codeine, and it can have some nasty side effects, like nausea and headache. Everyone was nice to me at home, my kids gave me cards and little presents, and in the evening when he came home from work, Larry gave me a beautiful card and money to buy myself a pair of boots I had wanted for a long time. It should have been a perfect day. I even plucked up my courage and rang my mum in the afternoon. She had emailed me the day before to tell me she wanted to ring me for my birthday and asked for my current phone number. For some reason I preferred to ring her before she did it. I always get a bit nervous when I talk to her.

Surprisingly, when I finally had her on the end of the line, I quite enjoyed it, maybe because I was still high on the tramadol I'd taken. She sounded quite positive about her cancer, which could be a façade, as I'm sure she must be quite shaken inside. But she doesn't like to show any weaknesses. She likes to prove she has full control over every aspect of her life. But I felt pleasure and relief talking with her, and she showed courage and determination when mentioning her diagnosis and upcoming chemotherapy. She said she would take it in its stride and make the most of it. She had even bought a wig to prepare herself for her first round of chemo. My mum has been through a lot with my dad, who had a bad temper when he drank, and I do admire her. She is brave and never complains about silly things like some other elderly people tend to do.

After that phone call, I felt drained and emotional. I needed to do something to keep going. I still had so much to do, shopping and getting Flynn's and Angie's lunchboxes ready for the next day, as well as making sure their school uniforms were clean and that they had socks to wear. I have done these things for years, but I still get stressed about the amount of work to do in a household with children and all the little details I need to pay attention too. Permission slips need to be signed, homework done and signed, water bottles filled, dinner prepared with nutritious food, protein, and vegetables. Then hot chocolate or Milo before bed, and bedtime reading with Angie … It's an endless routine, and sometimes I'm just fed up with it.

I was sick of doing all these things a mum does without thinking, never questioning her duties. My answer to the problem: to buy a packet of codeine painkillers. I went out and got one from the chemist. I took about eighteen tablets, as I was a bit scared of the combined effect with the tramadol that was already in my system. My premonition was correct. It was a disaster, worse than I had expected. That evening I felt fine; I was jumping around like a kangaroo, doing all my chores and feeling terrific. I went to bed relaxed and promising myself to give up all drugs the next morning.

On Wednesday I woke up feeling horribly sick. My head pounded so hard I was screaming, and I ran to the toilet several times to vomit water (I had hardly eaten anything the day before). I was in agony. I thought for a moment I was going to die. My husband and kids were worried, but I told them it was nothing, just a bad case of gastro. Everyone was on their best behaviour, tiptoeing around me and doing all they could so I was able to stay in bed. I slept for the whole day, and only got up feeling slightly better in the evening. I bought McDonald's for everyone. After preparing lunchboxes, I went back to bed, totally exhausted. I only ate dry biscuits and crackers because my stomach couldn't handle anything else. I fell into a deep sleep as soon as I went to bed at around 8 p.m. and woke up at 7:30 a.m. the next day to get Angie ready for school. Then I went back to bed again and slept until she came back from school. Finally in the evening, I felt better and vowed never to be so stupid again.

Today is day four, and I haven't had a craving for codeine. It is Saturday today, nearly midnight. I went out with Fiona and we took Angie with us. We went to the movies to see a chick flick that was appropriate for Angie. We had the best night ever. Larry stayed home and sorted out his clothes; then he played a game on his computer.

After Fiona left, I began writing this. Tomorrow will be day five. This time, I want to go for as long as I can without touching this dreaded substance. I hate it now, and I will hate myself even more if I put it into my body again. Thank God I haven't had any desire for it and I don't even want to think about it. I am asking for these painkillers to stay away from me once and for all. They're out of my life. Once they were my best friends, but now they're my worst enemies and I don't want to have anything to do with them anymore. And I won't allow work stress to get me down.

8 JUNE 2015

THIS MORNING I HAD AN argument with Larry about money—of course. It's always the same thing. He makes a lot more money than I do, but in my eyes he is stingy. I tried to explain to him that everything is expensive these days. Prices are not what they used to be. Groceries cost a fortune in Adelaide, and added to school fees and other costs, it's almost impossible to make ends meet. It's a constant struggle, and you need a tight budget. Now he wants to cut his contribution down because he thinks it doesn't reflect the reality anymore. I was outraged, but I gave up after a while. I can't be bothered arguing with him anymore. I wish I had married someone more generous, someone who could help me and support me better. Someone who feels for me when my washing machine breaks down, like it did yesterday. Now I have to buy a new one, and I don't know where to get the money. Larry said he wouldn't help me.

So this morning we had this argument, and I left the room almost crying. I didn't want to get upset, but it was too much for me. One day to the next is a battle for survival. And when unforeseen things happen, I lose my balance. I desperately wanted to go to the chemist to get some codeine painkillers. Then Georgia asked me to take her to the doctor's. She's been sick for a couple of days and complains about a sore throat and flu symptoms. I said okay, and off we went. Georgia's doctor is a lady, and I wanted to make an appointment with her. I don't know why, it was an impulse. The receptionist said to me, "Whey don't you go in today, just after Georgia? There is a spot available right after her." I agreed to do so, and when I saw her, I just burst into tears. I explained all my problems, feeling low all the time and without energy.

I told the doctor that I often take codeine painkillers for headaches, but I didn't tell her how many I usually take. I told her that ever since I decided to stop taking them, I'd been feeling depressed and anxious. I explained my lack of motivation and how I dreaded getting up in the morning. She listened empathetically and told me I was clinically depressed. She prescribed an antidepressant, venlafaxine, and told me to take it for at least two weeks without fail, then come back to see her and tell her how I feel. I explained to her how I had failed to take antidepressants in the past. After a few days, I would give up. She told me I had to give them a bit more time because the effect doesn't kick in straight away. You need to take them for at least four weeks to notice a difference.

I didn't tell Georgia anything about this. I just said to her I had some women's problems. On the way back, I called into the chemist to get my medication with the script the doctor had given me. I took a tablet before lunch time and started feeling a bit dizzy. My craving for codeine painkillers disappeared, and now it is almost 8 p.m., and I haven't had any desire for the drug all afternoon like I normally do, especially after a few dry days. So even if this doesn't work for depression, it might work to get me off codeine. That would be wonderful. I am determined to give it a go, and not give up after three days like I did in the past when on antidepressants.

According to online testimonies, venlafaxine works quite well, even though it has side effects like nausea, dizziness, and low libido, but it's important not to skip a dose, because withdrawals can set in right away and are quite unpleasant. I will do my best to take this medication as directed and on time, and maybe after I've been off the codeine for at least six months, I will stop it.

Anyway, it's day six today, and with this new plan, I stand a real chance to make it. The doctor also suggested counselling, and I think I will try it. I have done it in the past, so it's not the first time, but maybe it is time to discuss some issues. I don't feel unhappy as such. I am blessed with wonderful children and a decent husband, even if he's not the best husband. We have a roof over our heads, food on the table, and life is good. It's just in my head that things aren't going well. Perhaps I suffer from a brain dysfunction. Perhaps codeine painkillers were an attempt to self-medicate myself, who knows? I will find out in a few weeks on the new medication.

11 JUNE 2015

THE ANTIDEPRESSANT EXPERIMENT DIDN'T LAST long. I took the venlafaxine twice, but it made me sick and unable to function. The second time backfired. I went out to buy some codeine painkillers, simply because I felt terrible. I wanted something to make me feel better. At that moment, I didn't care. I just wanted to escape from this thick cloud that was obscuring everything. I felt so bad— shaky, nauseous, disoriented, unable to think coherently, and unable to concentrate.

My hands were unsteady, and I had trouble playing the piano. I can't go without playing the piano; it's one of the only things I enjoy. It takes my mind off my problems. I can take twenty-four codeine painkiller tablets and still play the piano. But with this antidepressant, I couldn't do it. That's why I decided to stop taking them right away. I don't have the patience to keep taking something that makes me feel worse. I don't know why that is the case. Maybe this particular type of antidepressant doesn't agree with me. I tried Prozac in the past, and it was much better than this medication.

Unfortunately, today I am back to day two, which is probably not a major setback. Yesterday I could have continued taking codeine painkillers. I still felt awful, but I decided not to do it. I thought about how bad I would feel the next day, and the next. I want to break this cycle once and for all. It's been going on for too long, for years. Why haven't I had the willpower to break this spell so far? The longest I've been able to go without these horrible tablets was two weeks. That was the year I turned forty-eight. Then I had a bad argument with Larry and started taking them again.

That wasn't the only time I tried to give up my addiction. Every time I tried to quit, something would happen and I would fall off the wagon. I have to control my emotions and be more laid back, less sensitive to everything. Why worry about silly things? Life is more important. I am alive today, and I am grateful for it, but if I go back to taking these painkillers, I will kill myself. This is what I need to realise, and I need to keep repeating it to myself.

Today I felt much better. After taking Angie to school, I played the piano, and my fingers felt light and nimble, like they haven't in a long time. My body was calm, and all tension had left. I'm not sure why. I haven't felt like that for a long time. Maybe I'm finally healing from my addiction. Wouldn't it be wonderful! There was a sense of peace in the air. My mind was focused, but my brain wasn't overloaded with thoughts as it usually is. I was still slightly anxious, but not to the point that it was a huge burden. I enjoyed my piano. The keys felt soft and sounded like crystal. It was pure pleasure to produce and enjoy the sound coming from them. It was like an eye opener, like I was playing for the first time.

Later on I went for a swim. Exercise is my cure, my salvation. If I can exercise on most days, I will have endorphins in my body, and I will be less likely to crave codeine. I would like to do yoga or Pilates two or three times a week and also swim at least twice a week. Swimming relaxes me more than any other activity.

In a way, I'm glad it didn't work out with the antidepressants. I didn't give them much time, but I can't stand feeling so sick that I'm incapacitated. And how would I have functioned at work? I even felt nervous getting into my car, scared I might have an accident. No, they aren't for me. I prefer to stick with natural stuff like St John's wort and Valerian. At least they don't have any frightening side effects.

I once wrote a script to hypnotise myself. That was about two and a half years ago. I found the piece of paper in a drawer, stumbling upon it yesterday as I was looking for a book I needed to give back to a friend. I will reproduce it here, as it is a good way to reinforce these intentions to myself. If I feel weak and tempted to go back to codeine painkillers, I want to read these affirmations to give me courage and keep me on the right path.

> I choose to put only natural, herbal remedies
> into my body.
> I have clean, clear, and healthy inner organs
> and my skin is glowing.
> I am in full control of my cravings and I only
> desire the things that are good for me.

My body is becoming healthier and healthier every day, as I continue to be free of chemicals.

I choose to take only natural medicines if I need to.

I deserve to be and I am now free of chemical painkillers.

I do everything without effort because my body is free of chemicals.

I now feel energetic, balanced, and optimistic all the time.

I look forward to my life and to the tasks ahead.

I enjoy the challenges life brings me.

I turn lemons into lemonade.

I am living a long and healthy life, totally free of my addictions.

I feel happier, at peace, and younger than I have ever felt before.

I look and feel great.

My body and mind are improving constantly, each day.

I enjoy eating fresh fruit and vegetables.

My body is cleansed and purified.

My body is now free of toxins.

The energy of wellbeing flows freely through my body and mind.

I am in total control of my life.

I choose to put only healthy things into my body.

I choose to enjoy good health and a long, happy, and productive life.

It's getting easier and easier to resist temptation.

I am determined in my goal to be healed.

I now smoothly sail through the storms of my life.

I can easily deal with ups and downs without losing my focus.

I choose good health and wellbeing all the time.

I am emotionally balanced and stable.

I am in control of my emotions at all times.

My thoughts are always positive.

I have peace and serenity in my life.

I am confident, secure, and content.

From the time I wake up in the morning, I look forward to every moment of the day.

I am always cool, calm, and collected.

I can handle situations in a mature and reasonable way.

I enjoy being the master of my destiny and the master of my emotions.

I am riding through great tumultuous moments with skill and assurance.

I am a beautiful, lovable, and valuable person.

I am very loving, patient, and forgiving.

I know how to set boundaries and to be firm when necessary.

I am strong and independent.

I love my family and I am doing this for myself and for them.

I am grateful to be alive and wish to live to be a hundred.

My cravings are now disappearing.

I am in control of what I am taking.

I know how to avoid things that are bad for me
and how to choose what is good for me.

I only use herbal health supplements and
vitamins.

My health is my priority—it comes before
everything else.

I choose a wholesome, healthy, proactive
lifestyle.

I stay away from toxic substances.

I always choose clean food and water.

This will be my course of action from now on.

I can do it—I am strong.

My weakness for this substance has vanished.

I am cured of my desire for them.

I am cured of my disease—I am well, body
and mind.

I am in harmony with the source of wellness
and the whole universe.

I am forever free and I love this newfound
freedom.

I have made a pledge.

I am profoundly disgusted with chemical
substances—they put me off.

I loathe touching them; I detest their side
effects.

I feel sick to my stomach at the thought of or at
the sight of one of these tablets.

I hate what they do to me.

I choose healthy alternatives from now on.

I know what I want and I stick by it, no matter what.

It is easy to implement my decision—it flows naturally.

I turn to meditation—it's better than medication!

When a craving arises, I use meditation and affirmations to overcome it.

My urges have flown away, never to come back.

I am enjoying this process—it's a miracle.

There is only peace, harmony, and ease in my life.

God looks after me—I am lucky.

I can do things easily and with pleasure.

It gives me pleasure to do chores and tasks I would normally find boring.

Stress is not part of my vocabulary.

I am excited as I am creating a new "me."

The new "me" is born. It is born to live!

I am free to do whatever I like, but I choose what is good for me, because that is what I want.

I persevere and I win. I am a winner!

I stick with my decision and I do what I say I will do.

I have strong willpower.

My imagination helps me to achieve my goal.

My imagination and willpower work in my favour and enable me to be who I want to be and to have what I wan to have.

All my useless guilt has evaporated.

I feel good and comfortable within myself.

I am at peace with myself.

It's okay to have a break when things get too much. Everyone needs a rest.

It's okay to have a "lazy" day.

It's okay to recharge my batteries when I need it.

The use of willpower improves my self-esteem and my self-image.

I can control myself so I can be myself.

20 JUNE 2015

TODAY IT SHOULD HAVE BEEN day eighteen since my birthday, but unfortunately it's only day two. Like so many times before, I'm back at the beginning, starting all over. I failed because of work. I know it's an excuse, but when last Friday came, over a week ago, I felt discouraged and weak, and I couldn't face going to work. I was scared I wouldn't be able to cope. I went for a couple of nights then called in sick. I don't know why I just couldn't face it. I had taken codeine painkillers and felt that if I continued working the remaining two nights, I would get worse and take more drugs. I knew they had strong codeine painkillers in the cupboard, but I didn't want to steal medications. I just don't want to do it anymore.

In a way this is progress, and I'm glad I've reached this point. I don't want to be a criminal. I might be everything else, but I don't want to go down that way anymore. I have done enough damage, mainly to myself, and I have lots of regrets and remorse. I know I can't undo the past and I will have to live with my mistakes, but at least I don't want to add more bad things to the list. The day I die and go to the other side, I will have a lot of explaining to do. I will probably spend years in purgatory, unless I find a way to amend myself in this lifetime. But I can't really see how. Maybe this is something I can worry about later, when I've been clean for longer than six or seven days.

Since yesterday I've been feeling a lot of self-hatred. I can't understand how I want to be a certain way, and yet I don't seem to be able to stick to what I've decided to do. It's an endless cycle of repeating the same mistakes over and over. I want to be free of painkillers, healthy, truthful, honest, and a good person, and yet whenever I try to be that way, I fail. I feel unworthy and a failure. I can't stand looking at my past; it seems so bad I want to erase it from my memory—years of living a life that is so contrary to my beliefs and to my ideals. I know I'm only a human, and we humans are not perfect. We are meant to make mistakes and learn from them. But in my case, I make a lot of mistakes, but I don't seem to learn anything. I start all over and repeat the same mistakes, without making any progress.

I am a total failure. This is how I feel right now, and I don't care what anyone says—that I shouldn't be so hard on myself. It's normal for me to feel bad, because I have done things that go against my own principles, not once but many times, and I have broken my own resolutions. Why is it that we humans decide on a course of action, but then do exactly the opposite? Is it so hard to make up your mind and stick by that decision once and for all?

How does the human brain make decisions? Your mind processes all the data it's given and comes out with the best possible choice, the one with the best possible outcome.

So how can you choose drugs versus staying clean, when drugs have so many negative consequences? The brain seems to conveniently bypass these consequences and only look at the pleasure gained from drug use. This is partial blindness, and it works by obliterating the destructive effects the drug has and highlighting the euphoria, the feeling of being on top of the world, the illusion that all is good, that I am a magnificent being who is loved and who loves everyone.

The drug gives you the illusion that you're in full control and that nothing can affect you, which is a lie, of course. The reality is so different. I wish I had more control over my life, my environment, and myself. My house is a mess. I don't have the energy to clean it. The garden is like the apocalypse. Larry doesn't help me fix it, that's true. But if he wasn't here I would have to do it too. I can't put all the blame on him.

No matter what, I'm starting all over again. I will never give up. Today is day two. I am confident I can do it, even though I have failed numerous, countless times. I will pick myself up again and give it another go. I don't care if my record proves I can't do this. I'm not here to prove anything, but to stay alive and look after my family. My children need me, especially Angie. I love her more than anything. She's the apple of my eye. I love all of my children, but Angie is the youngest and I feel more responsible for her. I feel that I need to be there for her and protect her. In the next ten years, I want to better myself, to change and become who I really am, a good person, and not a "fake" like I am now. I can't carry on hating myself if I want to achieve this.

Self-hatred will only lead me to punishment, and then I will be back to taking painkillers, because I despise myself and don't care about my health.

It just doesn't work. I need to let go of the past and forgive myself, even though it's the hardest thing. I never thought it would be so difficult to forgive myself, but today I know it is. It's much easier to forgive others for what they've done. After all, I don't have to live with them all the time, so it's easier to forgive and forget them. But I have to live with myself all the time, so how can I forget who I am and what I've done? True, I've never killed a human being, and I've never deliberately harmed anyone. But I've done enough to fill a book with my other sins, such as lying, cheating, and stealing. These are petty crimes perhaps, but awful and unforgivable in my own eyes.

Maybe the best way to get over a mistake is not to repeat it, and this is the only thing I can do. Guilt is a useless emotion. It does nothing to help, and it only leads to more mistakes. Guilt and punishment go hand in hand. Feeling guilt means more reasons to punish myself by making more mistakes. The cycle is complete, and guilt ultimately seals it and makes it bullet-proof. It forms a barrier around the past, encapsulating it and stopping the person from letting go of it and moving on to something better.

How do you let go of the past? By making the decision to let go, by expressing your feelings about it, acknowledging your responsibility. This is what I'm trying to do in these pages. I can stop to be a victim of my own circumstances and my own weakness. I can focus on the present, the here and now, the joy of being alive and being with my family. I can forgive everyone else, so I can forgive myself. I can stop judging myself. I can stop putting myself down and treating myself badly. I can have compassion and understanding for myself, while doing the best I can to be healthy. I can do it. I just need to believe in it, to believe in myself.

12 JULY 2015

IT'S BEEN THREE WEEKS SINCE I last wrote in this diary, and I'm not happy with myself. I have relapsed in a big way. I don't want to go into detail, as it is always the same story. I think I can handle this, so I say to myself, *I will only take six or eight tablets of codeine painkillers. No more. This is just to help me through the day.* Or through the night, or through whatever I can't handle at the time. Codeine painkillers are the remedy for all ills, for all unwanted emotions, for aches and pains in my body and in my soul. I think I can dictate my intake, how many tablets I will swallow, but then I soon spiral out of control.

This morning I felt awful. Yesterday between 4 and 6 p.m., I took eighteen tablets. Larry and I went out for dinner with some friends, Melody and Lance. Melody is my age, and Lance, who is her second husband, is fifteen years older, a few years older than Larry. We all got along well and enjoyed having dinner together. Yesterday was a perfect evening, and I felt wonderfully high, but no one noticed, because this is one good thing about codeine, no one notices any difference.

This kind of euphoria comes from the inside, but doesn't alter your behaviour. You're the same as usual, maybe just a bit more energetic and focused. I paid attention to our conversation and was a good listener to Melody, who has a lot of problems with her teenage daughter. I think we all felt grateful for that evening, even though the Indian restaurant food wasn't the best. I felt nauseous from it, but this is because I usually don't eat much fat. I eat very low fat, not because of my weight, but because it makes me feel better. So when I eat a meal high in fat, I almost become physically ill. But maybe it was also a side-effect from all the painkiller tablets I had taken before we went out.

When we arrived back home, Larry and I spent the rest of the evening doing stuff on the computer. I felt okay, nothing out of the ordinary. But when I woke up this morning, I thought I would die. I had such a bad headache I was screaming out in pain, crying and thrashing around in bed. I felt like vomiting, so Larry got me a bucket. I only vomited bile, and I was so weak I had trouble getting up to go to the toilet. I felt like this all day and ended up sleeping until 5 in the afternoon, only getting up to empty my bladder. I tried to drink as much water as possible to flush my system, and that helped. I was really scared that I had liver damage. What if my liver has finally packed up after all the abuse I have inflicted on it?

I might not drink any alcohol, but what I'm doing must be just as bad. I'm just in denial about it, I downplay it so it doesn't look as destructive, but it's not any better than being an alcoholic. It has to stop, or I will soon be dead, without a doubt. I have to stop right away. This is my last chance, regardless of withdrawal symptoms. I will have to put up with them, no matter what. Time is running out. Soon it will be too late. Today is the day and I will not go back anymore. No more codeine. Maybe I should try Prozac until I get out of this darkness, this cloud that is always surrounding me. Maybe I should just do it for six months.

As long as I can get off the codeine painkillers, that's the most important. I have no choice anymore, I have to hurry. I have to put all my efforts into this and win the battle against my demon. I can never take anything with codeine in it anymore, for as long as I live, or it will be the end of me. This is what I need to remember, all day, every day, from the time I get up in the morning until I go to bed and at night. God forgive me for this, I never meant to abuse myself in this way. The body is the temple of the soul, and I have violated it so many times. I am sorry.

17 JUNE 2015

I HAVE LASTED FIVE DAYS without using, and now it is day six. I really don't want to blow it this time. The last few days have been atrocious, with bad withdrawal symptoms: feeling sick to my stomach, nauseous, hot and cold, sweaty and restless at night. Right now I'm freezing cold and can't seem to warm up, even though I spent some time in front of the heater, attempting to soak up the heat. My hands are like ice blocks, which makes it hard to play the piano. I feel like doing nothing at all. I feel lazy, unmotivated, exhausted for no reason.

Last night I couldn't sleep. I was tossing and turning and getting up to go to the toilet every hour. I had restless legs and couldn't get comfortable, no matter what position I was in. I had to change my T-shirt three times as it was soaked in sweat. But when I removed my blanket I immediately felt the cold and had to put it back on. Thank God Larry didn't notice anything. He was fast asleep and I didn't want to disturb him, as he needs to get up early in the morning to go to work. I used a torch to go to the toilet, to avoid switching on the light. My bladder has been overactive this week; even when there is nothing in it I still feel the urge to go to the toilet.

I also worried that Larry had been snooping around my computer and discovered my diary. He talked about painkillers, and how the pharmacist asks you questions when you buy them, like "Are you on any other medication?" and "Do you know these can make you drowsy?" It was unnerving, as he only uses normal paracetamol or ibuprofen when he has a headache, nothing containing codeine. I hope he hasn't discovered my secret, as I don't want to share this with anyone. It's too embarrassing. I don't want to be judged by him, I don't want his help or his advice, and perhaps I don't want to look weak in his eyes. I'm scared of what would happen if he found out about it.

I wasn't very nice to Angie this morning. I had an argument with her and I regret it now. She didn't want to practice her piano. I reacted too much and got angry. She was upset and started crying. I feel awful about it now. Where has my patience gone? I am a ball of nerves, my mood is down, and I'm tired and irritable.

I went to see another doctor and asked him to put me on Prozac, because quite frankly I can't go on like this. I had Prozac in the past and tolerated it much better than venlafaxine (I will never try that drug again), and I also asked for some sleeping tablets. This goes against my principles, as I want to do everything the natural way. Valerian tablets don't seem to work for me anymore, and I need something to help me sleep as I don't want to go through sleepless nights while I wean myself off codeine painkillers.

I'm going cold turkey because it is the only way for me. Tapering down doesn't work for me. As soon as there is codeine in my bloodstream, I want more of it, so I find it easier to give it up altogether. I hate this addiction so much, but I love the feeling of inner calm and warmth that codeine can give me. I need to forget about it, to shut it out of my mind so I can move on. If I keep thinking about it and yearning for it, I will never kick this dangerous habit.

The physical withdrawals are bad, but the mental withdrawal is what has made me come back to this drug over and over. Now I understand what it feels like to be addicted to heroin, and I will never judge junkies anymore. You can have as much willpower as you want, it won't help you with opiates. Perhaps the only thing you can do is to keep trying, and this is what I will do, despite a strong desire to run to the chemist and ask for a packet of codeine painkillers, inventing some story about a headache that won't go away.

The addiction hijacks my thinking, making me believe that I am in control, when in reality I have no control over it. Two tablets, and I will be back to square one. It's not worth it. In the end I must admit that the codeine didn't give me much of a high. I was just taking it to feel *normal*, to keep functioning and to be able to cope with every day stresses. Now I feel empty, all my senses are alert, and I easily get startled when there is the slightest noise in the house. I feel like going into a padded room and sliding into oblivion. It's like I don't want to be here.

But I'm not suicidal. I want to live. I will pray to God for help and support. I have prayed a lot in the past but it didn't help. Maybe it will work this time. I'm so desperate. I try to distract myself as much as possible with reading, watching movies, and surfing the Net. Housework is not getting done and cooking is a thing of the past. Not very healthy for the kids, but I need to put myself first, so I won't worry about it for the time being. I just gave Angie two cut up apples to eat; at least she will get some fibre.

It's so hard to make decisions. I don't even know what to cook anymore; my mind is blank. Writing in this diary helps me, though. I was on the verge of giving in to my addiction, but I resisted. It's made me stronger. I'm fighting back. Withdrawal is painful, but the more I fear it, the stronger it becomes. I need to let it go and "ride the wave,'=" as they say, without giving in to these feelings. My mind plays tricks on me, urging me to continue with my addiction, but this is not what I want.

23 JULY 2015

I HAVEN'T MADE MUCH PROGRESS and I'm just trying to figure out why. My brain is fuzzy; I can't think clearly. Yesterday (Wednesday) I took ten codeine painkiller tablets, which is progress over Saturday when I took about twenty. It was horrible; I felt awful afterwards. I was at work, and on my break I was lying down on an empty bed and my head was spinning. I felt like I was having an out-of-body experience, but not a nice one.

Work is a problem for me, especially doing night shifts, because I tend to feel exhausted all the time, and this is how my addiction to codeine started in the first place. I noticed that codeine-based painkillers made me feel better. They allowed me to function in spite of fatigue. They took away the weariness, made me move around quicker, and made my brain sharper. I never got the drowsiness side-effects, just a feeling of calm and wellbeing, and the assurance of being able to cope with anything that was thrown at me. Nursing can be stressful. Unpredictable things can happen, like patients having falls or dying on your shift. It's not an excuse to become an addict, though. I'm just trying to make sense of this, and figure out why I've become this way, why I've become an addict.

This morning I felt discouraged, ready to give up, almost suicidal. I really don't want to go on living like this, fighting this addiction. I've had enough. I need help, but I'm not sure where to go. I feel tired, worn out, without the energy to go on. But I have to keep going, no matter what. There is no other way. My kids need me, especially the younger ones, Flynn and Angie. Georgia moved out to live with friends, and I am worried about her, but there isn't much I can do about it. It's her choice, and I respect it. At least she's not on drugs.

Georgia's friends are Christians and they go to church together, which is reassuring, even though there are no guarantees. She came home for a visit the other day, and while she was on the computer, I opened her handbag to have a snoop. I know it's not the right thing to do, but I'm her mum after all. I found an opened packet of cigarettes in her bag, and I nearly choked. I couldn't say anything to her, and I know that even if I did, it wouldn't make much difference. Then again I used to smoke when I was her age, so how can I tell her not to do it? How can I tell anyone what to do when I have this addiction myself? I'm not a good role model. And I've also become lazy. I hardly do any housework anymore, just the minimum. I don't have the motivation to do anything.

Going back to Saturday when I fell off the wagon, I know it had something to do with Friday. On Friday I went to the doctor and asked him to put me on Prozac. I took a tablet the same day and felt slightly better, but then at work I started to feel bad. I tried to close my eyes and doze off like I usually do on my break, around 2 in the morning. I couldn't relax; I was restless, and sleep evaded me. I took half a tablet of lorazepam, a calmative that I found in the pharmacy box. I fell asleep, but on waking up I felt awful. At home I had a good sleep for several hours, but when I woke up I felt terrible again and went to buy a packet of codeine painkillers (twelve tablets). That was at around 5 p.m. I felt much better, but it wasn't enough, so I bought another packet of twelve before I went to work. I took eight tablets out of it. So altogether I took twenty tablets.

I felt like a failure, but I was able to function at work, even though I was overcome with guilt and shame. The following night I went back to work and I did much better as I didn't take any codeine painkillers. I was happy with myself. I've never gone to work without taking codeine painkillers first. This has been going on for years. At least now I know that I can cope without. It was difficult, trying to focus and do all my work without the help of this chemical crutch, but I've proved to myself that I can do it. It's something I can cling to. It gives me some reassurance that I can go to work clean and cope relatively well. I usually have no motivation and no drive, but now I know that I can get through the night without codeine painkillers.

I used to love nursing, but after years of doing it I feel burnt out, and I dislike it now. I don't feel any enthusiasm for it anymore, but I still do the best job I can, as I feel empathy for the elderly and would never treat them with disrespect. But the truth is that for a long time now, I've been doing my job solely for the money. It's hard to keep going, but I have to, for my children's sake. I have to pay for Flynn's private school fees and his sports lessons, as well as Angie's extra-curriculum activities. Brandon loves tennis, and Angie does gymnastics, piano, and horse-riding. It costs me a fortune. I have to pay for food and half of the household bills. Larry doesn't realise how much things cost. Groceries cost a fortune in Adelaide. To this add the children's clothes, school uniforms, tennis rackets and balls, gymnastic clothes, and horse-riding gear. The list is endless. Sometimes I don't know how I'll survive. I used to shoplift sometimes, but now I don't do it anymore, I'm scared of getting caught and I feel guilty about it. I don't want to be a thief anymore. I don't want to be a criminal and end up in jail.

I have to keep working unless I win the lotto. That would be nice, and I would like to think it could happen. At least I wouldn't have to worry about money, and I could concentrate on giving up my addiction and getting healthy. I've always wanted to be healthy, and it's as if that goal has escaped me ever since I pursued it, from the time I was a teenager. I had eating disorders, then later turned to alcohol and cigarettes. I think the only times of my life when I was really healthy were during my pregnancies. I was too scared to take anything because I didn't want to cause birth defects to my babies. It's a shame I can't be pregnant continuously (I'm joking of course). At least I'd be too frightened to take codeine painkillers!

I'm back to square one, and this time I need to focus on what helped me stay away from these tablets in the past. Prozac doesn't work for me, obviously. It makes me feel so bad that I go back to taking codeine painkillers. It makes me feel as though I can't think and concentrate properly. I will have to accept my depression and deal with it; there is no other way. Does the depression stem from my addiction or did I become addicted because I was depressed? I don't know anymore. It's like the question about the chicken and the egg—which one came first?

I've always had a lot of anxiety and intrusive thoughts, feelings of impending doom and catastrophe. I'm terrified something might happen to my children. But these feelings are not new, and I know they are irrational. I've had a phobia of cancer for a long time, ever since I was sixteen years old, which is much better now, probably because I don't care if I die anymore. But I wouldn't like to have cancer, though. I wouldn't like to die; I still have a lot of living to do. But I want to live free of addiction and free of withdrawal and craving. I just want to be *normal*. Is this an impossible goal? And if it's not impossible, why is it eluding me?

I need to keep writing in this diary. It seems to be the only thing that helps. It allows me to express my feelings and obtain some clarity about what's happening to me. I'm going to have a new attempt at giving up my drug of addiction, keeping in mind all the things that have helped me in the past: exercise, prayer, meditation, natural remedies, and just sticking with it, no matter what. I'm not going to die from withdrawal or craving. It's just something I need to handle better.

I might need help, but I'm not sure where to go. If only I could talk to someone who understands. I don't want to be judged or looked down upon. I know a lot of this is my fault, and I take responsibility for it. But I don't want it rubbed in my face. I feel bad enough as it is. My only wish is to overcome this addiction and share my experience with others to help them. This would be a good life purpose, something to give to other people in the same situation.

It looks so bleak when you're in the middle of it, and there seems to be no way out. Life doesn't seem to be possible without the crutch of codeine painkillers. It's hard to imagine there is light at the end of the tunnel, and that there is a life beyond the mental and physical pain of addiction. As long as I keep writing in this diary, I feel that I'm on the right track.

3 AUGUST 2015

IT'S BEEN OVER A WEEK now since I last wrote in my diary, and I don't have any good news. I relapsed, taking twenty-four tablets of codeine painkillers every day or every second day on average. Whenever I try to stop, I get really bad withdrawal symptoms. I just can't function, and I'm overcome with such a strong craving for the drug that I can't resist jumping into my car and driving to the closest pharmacy to obtain my supply. I'm basically at the end of my tether. I don't want to know what damage I'm doing to my body, I just can't face it. I keep living in denial. I don't want to face reality.

I am fifty years old and I don't want to die. I want to live to a hundred, to see my children have children and see my grandchildren grow up. I don't want to exit this stage now. But if I continue this way, I won't be here for much longer. I won't be here for those I love: Daniel, Fiona, Georgia, Flynn, and Angie. I won't be there to enjoy retirement with Larry, if I'm still with him by then—who knows? I will let everyone down and destroy their lives. I should live well into my eighties and nineties and possibly hundreds, if only I could take care of myself properly, take care of my body and stop abusing it.

Things are now out of my hands. My life has become unmanageable. I am a mess, but everyone thinks I'm all right. No one knows about my lonely secret. I need to do something urgently to break out of this jail, to put an end to the vicious cycle of abuse. I desperately want to quit, but then I succumb to overwhelming cravings. It's like I can't control my brain. I can't focus without my drug. Without it, I feel lethargic, depressed, depleted of energy, without motivation. I just want to curl up in bed and sleep all day, which I have been doing lately when the kids are at school and Larry is at work. I don't get anything done, just lying in bed and escaping into sleep. I can't face my life; it's too difficult. When I take codeine painkiller tablets, I can get things done. I'm effective: I can do my housework, shopping, cooking. And I can go to work when I have night shifts.

If only I could rewind my life to a time when I wasn't addicted, when I didn't know what codeine could do for me. I want to go back to who I used to be. My life wasn't perfect, and I had problems, but I wasn't a painkiller junkie. I was a normal person trying to cope. Even when the children were little, I was doing well. I remember that things were extremely stressful at times; the kids were demanding, like toddlers and babies normally are. But I attended to their needs, I looked after them, I gave them all my love. I wasn't always as patient as I wished I were, but on the whole I was doing a good job as a mum.

I didn't try to escape from a reality that was too hard to bear. I didn't attempt to feel different, to get high on drugs. Now this is all I want to do, even though I tell myself it's wrong. I want to be somewhere else, in a world of perfection and bliss. I've had enough of doing the same things over and over again. The same chores: cooking, washing, cleaning, grocery shopping, and then going to work at night, when I should be asleep in bed.

We are going away at the end of this month, and I am terrified. We are going to Europe, Larry, Flynn, Angie and I, to visit my mum, who paid for our tickets (except for Larry's). She's been diagnosed with breast cancer but refuses chemotherapy. It might be the last time I see her. I hope not, and I cling to the possibility that her immune system will beat the cancer without the help of chemicals. It's quite possible, because my mother is a very strong woman who's in control of her life. She makes a point of being healthy in every way, and she looks after her body to the point of obsession. Perfection means a lot to her, and she won't allow herself to have any extra weight. She exercises at least two hours every day and eats a balanced diet. My mum has never been overweight or out of shape. She has very high expectations of herself, and she used to expect a lot of her daughters too when we were growing up. My sisters and I had a lot of psychological problems.

I've decided to go and see a doctor tomorrow, to own up to my problem. I want the doctor to help me and put me on something like Suboxone, a replacement drug, or on a codeine tapering-down programme. This means I would start with my normal dose of codeine, and every day take a little less, until I'm down to nothing. This way I wouldn't experience these awful withdrawal symptoms. I read about it on various forums on the Internet, and it seems to be the best solution. Suboxone is a drug they give to junkies to stop them from using, but it doesn't make you high. It just keeps withdrawal and cravings at bay, which is what I need. I will ask the doctor what he or she thinks is best for me, Suboxone or a progressively smaller dose of codeine every day. It's a doctor I have never met before. I wouldn't be able to confess to my regular doctor, as he believes that I'm a healthy and positive person, and it would be so embarrassing to admit the truth to him.

6 AUGUST 2015

THE VISIT TO THE DOCTOR on Tuesday was a complete waste of time. The same day I went to the chemist to get my supply of codeine painkillers. The doctor didn't take me seriously. Maybe he thought I was an attention seeker. Anyway, the next day I did the same thing; I bought a packet of painkillers, even though I vowed not to do it. I don't think he could understand the depth of my addiction and my desperation. To most people, it boils down to willpower alone. I believe I actually do have a lot of willpower, but the addiction is stronger. It is insidious and gets into my brain. I want to do one thing, which is to remain clean and drug-free, but then I do the opposite; I act against my own will, my own resolutions. I go back to my addiction, and I have no idea why. It's as if I tell my brain something, but my body does something different. I act like a robot, as if on automatic pilot. It's as if things are out of my conscious control. No one can understand this.

The doctor gave me a kind of a pep talk, which I listened to politely, but it did nothing for me. I've read so many self-help books, I know everything about positive thinking and positive self-talk in front of the mirror. It's nothing new to me. I can be the most positive person ever, and it won't change anything. The addiction is stronger. The urge to take codeine painkillers overrides everything. I wanted to doctor to give me a replacement drug, like Suboxone or codeine tablets, so I could slowly taper off my intake. But he only gave me a prescription for Valium.

As I left the surgery, I went to the chemist and handed in my prescription. They gave me a bottle of fifty tablets of Valium 5 mg. I took one tablet straight away and felt lethargic and out of this world. I hate that feeling of not being in control. I can't stand this drug, how it makes me feel drowsy. I just want to be able to function, and this does the opposite. I couldn't function at all and became unfocused and clumsy. That's why I had to drive to another pharmacy and get a packet of my usual codeine painkillers. I took twelve tablets in one go and felt better right away. My brain came back to life. I could do all the chores I had to do. I felt on top of the world. But my addiction was still there, and the doctor hadn't helped me. Valium is not going to get rid of it.

He also ordered me to take a blood test, which I reluctantly did. I'm so scared. What frightens me the most is the damage I must have done to my body with all this abuse. I did the test, though, I don't know why. I was going to leave the surgery, but I was literally pushed into a room and this lady took my blood. She was very chatty and overly friendly, which I found a bit inappropriate. It's okay to be chummy, but in this setting you expect someone to be professional and reassuring. It's not like we're at a party of having a social get-together. But she did a good job, as I didn't feel any pain, which is a good sign as my veins are small and not many people are able to insert a needle into my arm without several botched attempts and a lot of discomfort for me.

My pain threshold is very low, and I react to the slightest feeling of discomfort with emotion. Maybe this is part of why I became addicted to painkillers. They make me less raw, less sensitive. And with all the traumas from my first failed marriage, then my present marriage that was on the rocks for a long time before things began to settle down. Sometimes I think I may suffer from post traumatic stress disorder. I'm sure that if I could discover the real reason behind my addiction, I would get better. I need to dig within myself and uncover the truth.

Today I feel fine, although I'm very tempted to go out and get my supply of drugs. But I won't give in. I always feel exhausted. I have no energy during the day and I've had enough. I want to feel better, not so tired all the time. I can't stand this constant feeling of lethargy. I want to have the up-and-go I used to have. I want to wake up in the morning and feel good. It's been ages since that happened. I just long to be normal, and yet I doubt it will ever happen. I only appear normal because I can find all sorts of excuses. For instance, I tell my family I'm tired because of the night shifts I do. I tell them it takes a long time to get over the fatigue. I wish I could go back in the past and be the person I used to be, ten or twelve years ago. I had my life under control.

Back then, my weight was stable. I looked great in jeans. I wasn't depressed. I used to look forward to things, even though my life wasn't always easy and things were pretty bleak at times. But I wasn't taking painkillers, even though

I drank alcohol occasionally, maybe once a month at the most. I sometimes needed to "drown my sorrows" due to my problems with my ex-husband Brett. He often drank excessively and went out all night while I waited for him at the kitchen table. This lasted for years, as I always hoped things would get better. But he ended up having an affair with another woman. He said he didn't love me anymore and moved out, leaving me on my own with four children.

Tomorrow I'll get the results of my blood test. I will know what damage I've done to my body. I don't want to continue doing this. I know I can stop, if only I have enough courage and determination to do it. And I need help but I don't know where to get it. I need to think and make a decision. I'm sure there are places where I can get the help and support. I need to overcome this terrible addiction. It's a lonely secret, because I've allowed it to be that way. Once I start talking about it and sharing it, it won't be a secret anymore, and it might lose its power over me. I have allowed this addiction to grow strong because I've kept it hidden. It's time to take the lid off this dirty secret and stop being ashamed about it. Guilt and shame won't do anything to help me, but openness and acceptance will. I haven't lost hope.

7 AUGUST 2015

MAYBE THIS IS A WAKE-UP call for me. I went back to the doctor's and he looked at my blood results and saw that my liver enzymes were up. This means the beginning of liver disease, the sign my liver cells are damaged by the painkillers I've abused. The doctor said it was reversible because this is only the early stage, and if I stop doing what I'm doing right away, I will be fine. So now I have no excuses anymore. I don't want to die of liver cirrhosis. I might not be a drinker, but this is just as bad.

All my other results are okay, except for cholesterol, which is a bit high. Perhaps this is because my liver isn't working properly. Also, my iron is low and I think it's because I've been abusing codeine painkillers. I'm sure it affects your iron levels. The doctor was puzzled because I am menopausal and I haven't had my period for over a year now. He wanted me to do a test for occult blood, which means they analyse your faeces to see if there is any hidden blood in it, just in case you're bleeding from the inside, like from the stomach or the intestine. I don't think I will bother with it. It was scary enough doing the blood test and finding out the result. If I have some kind of internal bleeding, I'd rather not know about it. I have enough to worry about.

I'm just grateful my kidneys are still functioning properly. Maybe it's because I drink so much water. I'm always scared of damaging my kidneys, as I have seen people on dialysis and it's not a nice thing. But liver cirrhosis is equally scary, maybe even more. A slow deterioration and a long painful death. An abdomen inflated like a balloon or like a nine-months pregnant woman, full of ascites (an accumulation of fluid in the peritoneal cavity).

I may have only reached day two so far, but this is the end of my over-the-counter codeine-based painkiller addiction. I needed to be shocked into it, so my common sense can finally triumph over this stupid behaviour. Because it's only a behaviour, nothing more, and behaviour can be modified. Fear can do wonders when willpower has been ineffective. Someone with a diagnosis of lung cancer is more likely to give up smoking than someone who is perfectly well and has no negative side-effects from smoking. So in a way I'm glad this happened; it will motivate me to give up my addiction once and for all.

I didn't expect to be in perfect good health, as I've been abusing my body for a long time. I'm very lucky I haven't damaged anything besides my liver. The liver is a terrific organ, and it does recover, from what I understand, unless you've got cirrhosis, which is irreversible. There is hope if I totally abstain from my drug from now on. I can't go back to this insanity. It's too late. If I do, I might as well call myself suicidal.

I told the doctor I didn't like the Valium he prescribed for me, as it makes me sleepy. He said that if I needed something else like Suboxone, I should go to the Drug and Alcohol Rehabilitation Centre. I don't really want to go there. That would be the last straw, and from then on I would really call myself a junkie. I don't want to be around these people. I'm so ashamed of where this addiction has taken me. I know I should open up about it, but right now I want to deal with it on my own, and knowing the result of my blood test will force me to stay on track. I don't have a choice anymore.

Tonight I'll go back to work and I'll think hard about what kind of meaningful career I could pursue instead of aged care nursing. The stress of my job and the tiredness of doing night shifts precipitated my addiction to painkillers. But what else could I do? Ideally, I would like to help children, become a foster parent, but I need a proper job too. Night shifts are horrible. They've made me relapse many times, when I've managed to stay clear of painkillers for some days. Shift work is not good for me, yet I can't think of anything else I could do that pays well enough that I can support my children and pay the bills. But I don't want to kill myself just for money.

13 AUGUST 2015

I'M A NERVOUS WRECK. I was caught shoplifting twice, within two days! I don't know why I did it. It was an impulse and I gave in to it. I feel so guilty and ashamed, and I'm afraid everyone will judge me and look down upon on me and treat me like a low-life. Hatred is all I deserve. It's a wake-up call, a warning never to do this again.

The first time I was apprehended by two plain-clothed loss prevention officers at the supermarket checkout, after paying for my groceries. I had hidden some in my bag. They took me to a little office at the back of the store. It was dark and depressing, with a computer on an old desk and a few decrepit chairs. They made me sit down and asked me to give a statement, after giving me a big lecture on what I did and why it was wrong. I agreed with everything they said. I told them I was very sorry and would never do it again.

I said I had problems at home and was depressed. It was an impulse, as I was overcome with a strong urge to take some items without paying for them. It was no excuse, and it was the wrong thing to do. In the end I cried, and the detectives were quite nice and understanding, and not too harsh. They said I just escaped a big fine of $500 on the spot, only because the amount of my stolen goods was under $100. I breathed a sigh of relief. I would be banned from the store for six months. I was shaken after that experience, and a normal people would not do it again, but I don't know what's wrong with me.

The next day I did it again. I went to a different supermarket and took some items off the shelves and put them into my bag, just stupid things like mouthwash, a packet of biscuits, coffee, chocolate powder, and potato crisps. It wouldn't have amounted to more than $35. I don't know what got into me, even though it's not the first time. Am I a kleptomaniac, or is it because I'm depressed? I know it's so silly and risky, as well as evil, but when it happened, I couldn't stop myself.

When I went through the self-serve checkout, the lady asked to have a look inside my bag. I panicked and said I was in a hurry. I walked away quickly without turning around. She was shouting, which was embarrassing. I hope that there wasn't anyone in the store who knew me. While she yelled at me hysterically, I slipped out to the car park and went into my car. I turned around and spotted another store employee jotting down my number plate. Terrified, I was shaking all over.

Now I'm scared the police will come to my door and arrest me. I'll have to go to court and get a fine or even a police record. All these things can happen. They might have me on camera. They might have proof that I stole the goods, with my face in plain evidence. I don't know what to do, but I can't talk about it to anyone.

When I came home I was trembling, and I sat down in a daze. I couldn't do anything. I was supposed to go to a piano lesson with Angie in the afternoon, but I rang the teacher and told her I couldn't make it. I drove to her place to pay her and started crying when I was there and she gave me a hug, but I couldn't tell her what was wrong. It was awful. Then I drove to the nearest chemist and bought a packet of thirty codeine painkillers, and I swallowed them all. I felt terrible.

Later on that day I had an argument with Larry about things that are unresolved in our relationship. But he wouldn't listen to my point of view, and I became upset. I'm so sick of him sometimes. He doesn't understand how I feel. He wants everything his way, and when things go wrong, he blames me for it. I want to walk away from him and be free. I can't stand this situation any longer. Now I have to stop writing because he came home from work, and he might look over my shoulder to see what I'm writing.

17 AUGUST 2015

I HAVEN'T TOUCHED ANY CODEINE products since Wednesday so that makes it four full days, and today is number five. I went back to the doctor's since I wanted to do something about my depression, if that's my problem. I guess it might be, or else why would I do stupid things like shop stealing and taking entire packets of codeine painkillers? There must be something wrong with me.

On Friday, I was anxious, sick with fear about my shoplifting, so I paid $80 to a website and submitted this question to a solicitor:

"I shoplifted at a store, ordinary groceries to the value of around $45. I am fifty years old, and I suffer from depression. I know it's no excuse, and I will never do it again. I feel very guilty and ashamed. So I just put these items into my bag and as I went through the checkout, the sales assistant asked me to show her what was inside my bag. Unfortunately, I panicked and I said I was in a hurry. This is because I thought I saw someone I knew behind me in the shop watching me, and I didn't want to be spotted by this person. I began walking away quickly, while the checkout lady was yelling in a high-pitched voice. I went to the car park and just as I got into my car, I noticed another store employee writing down my number plate on a notepad. I must admit I have taken a few items from that store on previous occasions, so they might have me on camera. I don't want any lectures, as I realise my mistakes. I know this is wrong, and against the law. But now I live in fear. This happened two days ago and I am terrified of getting arrested."

And this is the answer I received shortly afterwards from a solicitor called Paul:

"Even if you will be arrested, the police will likely not charge you, I suggest going back to the store and arrange payment of $50 for the groceries that were taken.

If you are charged, it is likely that a magistrate will dismiss the criminal charges considering that you suffer from depression and have not been charged with anything familiar in fifty years."

I found the answer a bit short, but it was to the point and it made me aware I needed to arrange for counselling. I need to do something about my depression. I will do it when I come back from Europe. The doctor also gave me Stillnox to help me sleep and I have taken Prozac for two days now and it seems to keep my cravings for codeine at bay. I know it's not really what I want because I'd rather only take natural products. But it's better than overdosing myself with painkillers and destroying my liver.

I worry a lot about my liver. I might continue on Prozac for a little while, until the codeine is completely gone from my system and I don't have a need for it anymore. I don't know if it makes me feel better. At least I can function. I got out of bed and didn't go back to bed when Angie went to school, as I have been doing lately. My daughter Georgia just arrived and wants to go for a swim, so we will go to the swimming pool together.

Yesterday morning I had diarrhea, probably from codeine withdrawal. It was annoying, but I didn't allow it to deter me. I don't have a choice in this anymore. I have to be strong. I'm leaving for Europe in twelve days and I *have* to be clean. I can't allow this to interfere with my plans. If the police charge me with shoplifting, I will plead guilty, but use my depression as an "excuse." I know it's not good, but if I need to be punished, they will decide to do it. I've made a lot of bad choices, but hopefully I can better myself in the future. I can decide to stay on the right track and stick to my resolution to quit painkiller drugs forever.

On Friday I had lunch with my best friend Melody and it was really nice. The conversation flowed well. We talked about everything, except my addiction. I can't open up about it, especially not to Melody, I don't know why. I should trust her, though, as I've known her for over twenty years. I find it hard to talk about myself, to be honest about what I really am. I come across as confident, as someone who copes well with everything, but on the inside it's a different story. I enjoyed being with Melody though and meeting up at the restaurant. It made me realise I need to socialise more. I need to be more normal, not try so hard all the time. I need to relax and be myself.

21 AUGUST 2015

THIS IS NOW DAY NINE without painkillers, without any codeine containing products at all. I have never been that long without this drug before, only once about two years ago when I went for two weeks, then relapsed when I returned to work on night shift. This time, I swear I will not relapse. The Prozac helps a bit, but I don't like the effect of it on my brain, even though it seems to keep me in line. It's affecting me in a negative way. I can't explain how. I'm just not feeling like I am myself. This might also be due to lack of sleep. Sleep has eluded me for the last few days. I will stop taking Stillnox. I was popping one tablet as prescribed before bed, end even though it did put me to sleep for a few hours, I was waking up in the early morning hours without being able to go back to sleep. I feel tired and jittery as a result.

I have a lot of housework and cooking to do because I have two Japanese exchange students staying with us. They're really nice, but very shy and polite and they don't express their needs. That makes it hard for me, as I need to guess what they want. Their knowledge of English is minimal, and we need to use a translator app on my smart phone to communicate effectively. I don't mind having them here, but I feel stressed. It means having breakfast and dinner ready by a certain time. I have to prepare packed lunches for them. They go to a local high school, but not the same one as Flynn's. I have to drive them there in the morning and pick them up in the afternoon. Flynn catches the bus to his school. It's all getting a bit too much for me. A lot of running around, but I'm still coping so far. I've been doing it since Monday when they arrived, and by now I'm exhausted. At the same time, it is keeping me busy and my mind is not wandering towards codeine.

Their culture is so different from ours. They truly respect older people and authority. But they're also a lot more pampered than our kids, especially being boys, and won't take any initiative. You even have to tell them to have a shower, or they won't do it. You have to tell them everything! It can be quite daunting, and I don't know how I will manage this weekend since I also have to work. I hope I will survive.

Our trip to Europe is also coming closer: We're leaving next Friday. I talked to my mum on the phone the other night, and she seemed positive and looking forward to seeing us. I haven't seen her since 2001, when she came to visit us in Australia. I was still married to Brett back then. That seems ages ago. Our trip is only one week away. I will need to pack for Angie, Flynn, and myself. I was thinking about buying enough underwear and socks for three weeks and throwing them out as we go to avoid having too much washing.

Talking about my addiction, I think negative motivation works better than positive expectation. I always thought the opposite was true. But ever since I found out my liver results were high and that I'm in danger of liver damage, I feel more motivated to give up this horrible drug. I never want to go back to it. I have decided I want to live, no matter what, and I want to get better. I want my liver results to go back to normal within the next three weeks, if possible. That's my goal. I might still take Prozac for a little while, but I want to stop that as well. I just want to be *myself* again, whatever that means. All my live, I've been healthy. Even though I might not have been as healthy as I wished to be, I was well. My blood tests were always normal. Only this time it was different, and it is scary. *Fear* is probably the greatest motivator.

Nine days is a very long time for me, and this time going back to work is not going to deter me from my goal. It's not going to make me go back to codeine painkillers. It's such a dangerous, addictive substance. I think it should be banned from over-the-counter sales. Just the other day I was at the chemist, buying a nasal decongestant (one of the withdrawal symptoms from codeine seems to be a stuffy nose) and a young woman was asking for a packet of codeine painkillers, the same brand I usually buy. I felt sorry for her, and instantly I felt like warning her about the danger of this drug. But I couldn't say anything. I guess people have to go through their own process of getting addicted, until they realise what this medication has done to them. It can ruin your life. It can even kill you. I'm lucky it hasn't killed me. I won't let that happen. I'm removing it from my brain, so my thought won't go back to it all the time. It's not about being strong anymore. It's about staying alive.

26 AUGUST 2015

I WOULD BE HAPPY IF I could say that I passed the two weeks' mark without a relapse. Unfortunately, it's not the truth. I fell off the wagon badly, and I'm trying to figure out why. Maybe there is *no* excuse, and I just need to try harder. Looking back on the past two weeks, I find that taking Prozac was a big mistake. It made me incapable of sleeping naturally. Inevitably, I needed something to make me sleep. That's why I took Stillnox every night. At the end of the week (by Friday) I was a nervous wreck, even though I believed I wasn't. I thought I was doing fine, when in reality, I was sabotaging myself and working towards a relapse. I have since thrown *all* my tablets in the garbage bin.

On Saturday morning, while I was at work, I took some tramadol capsules I found in the pharmacy return box (drugs that go back to the pharmacy). It was a mistake. Straight away, it took me back to square one. I was *hooked* again. A little while later, I felt compelled to take some more tramadol that night. Then I did the same thing again on Sunday morning. I also took some home with me "in case I needed them," and swallowed them on Saturday afternoon, just "to keep me going."

We took our two Japanese students to the beach and to eat sushi. It was a good day, and they had a great time, enjoying the scenery and the food. We were all happy. Then things took a bad turn. After we got home, I had an argument with Larry. He had forgotten his wallet before we left. While at the restaurant, I said I would pay for everything, as long as he agreed to transfer some money back to me later, half of the bill, which is an unspoken agreement which he usually follows, that we split all the bills in half. We do this for the household bills too, electricity, gas, water, rates, and so on.

But when we arrived home, he suddenly changed his mind. He told me I had to give him money instead. I was shocked. I didn't know why he said that, seeing that I'd paid for our meal at the Japanese restaurant. I felt devastated and started crying. I shouted at him, even though I didn't mean to. I didn't really care about the outcome of the argument, I don't know why. The tramadol I'd taken lingered in my system, making me robot-like and dispassionate. Whether I won the argument or not didn't matter to me anymore. The next morning he changed his mind and was more amicable. Maybe he thought about it during the night. This is how things work with him. He needs time to think things through, and I need to be patient. He agreed to pay me back some of the money, and he even gave me *more* than I'd expected. He offered to pay for over half of the meal. I don't like arguments, but sometimes it's good to stick up for yourself. As long as things don't get out of control and degenerate into a nasty argument, expressing your point of view can clarify things and achieve results.

On Sunday night, I was exhausted and called in sick at work for Sunday and Monday night. I couldn't do those shifts, because it meant taking *more* drugs. I couldn't put myself through that anymore. I wanted to be clean again, but how? By now the tramadol I'd taken had affected me badly. It's a horrible drug. It leaves you with a dreadful hangover. You feel bad for a day or two afterwards.

On Monday I felt terrible, so I bought some codeine painkillers from the pharmacy. My daughter Georgia came over for a visit, and I found some stronger codeine painkiller tablets in her bag. I took some of those, only leaving a couple of them in the packet. I was ashamed. How can you take tablets from your own daughter? How low do you need to go, to take medicines from your own daughter's prescribed supply?

This addiction turns me into a person without morals and without scruples. On the outside, I appear to be a caring, compassionate, loving, smiling person and a devoted mum. If only people saw the real picture, the raw truth. They would get a shock. They would not want to be around me anymore. I have so many things going for me, and yet I destroy what I have. I don't look after myself, I put rubbish into my body, and now my liver is probably permanently damaged because of it. How can I get out of this vicious cycle, how can I escape from this downward spiral and make my way up again?

I have gone back to basics. It is day two for me. The Japanese students left yesterday. It was getting stressful for me having them in the house, cooking and doing their washing and ironing and entertaining them too. Even though I enjoyed hosting them, I will not do it anymore. It's too much for me, and I'm feeling so much more relaxed now that they've left. I'm trying to take it as easy as possible. No piano, no swimming, no going crazy trying to achieve things and feeling bad if I can't. I just went shopping for cat food and litter this morning, as we will be away for three weeks and there has to be enough for the cats and their kittens.

Our beautiful Siamese female cat Stella recently had four kittens, and they're so cute! We own the father too. He is a pure Siamese cat with a pedigree. His name is Picasso, and he is an absolute sweetheart. I plan to sell the kittens as soon as they're ready to be adopted by good families. I would like to keep them all, but that's impossible. I also need the extra money. I don't know why I'm constantly financially insecure, even though I always seem to manage somehow. I always have a feeling something's going to happen, that I won't be able to pay for my bills of for food. If only I had a better income, I wouldn't worry so much.

I still haven't received anything in the mail from the police regarding my embarrassing shoplifting incident. Maybe I got away with it, which I don't deserve. I suppose they don't bother with petty thieves like me, who take a packet of sugar and tea bags and a bottle of vitamins pills. They have more serious crimes to solve.

There is a big "ice" problem in Adelaide. There are methamphetamine labs everywhere, according to the media. People must have been watching too much *Breaking Bad*. At least I've never touched illegal drugs in my life. Every drug I've ever taken was legal. I'm just an ordinary mum. I just wish I was stronger, and I had more willpower.

I need to get on top of this now. I read somewhere that the desire to quit a drug must be as strong as the desire to take the substance was in the first place. I think the desire to quit must be *stronger* than the desire to take the drug. Or else it won't be possible. If I still crave the drug and long for it, I won't be able to stay clear of it. I need to take it out of my mind and stop thinking about it, once and for all. It's not an option for me anymore. I have to cope with things in a different way.

For instance, I worry a lot about money and I'm terrified of not having enough of it, or of losing my job. And yet I take a lot of sick days, which doesn't make much sense. I should work more if I want more money. It's just that I don't want to keep taking drugs, so I avoid doing shifts because it's one of my triggers. It stresses me out so much that I don't know what to do. I'm constantly overwhelmed by all the things I need to do. It's a vicious cycle, never-ending and overwhelming. I hope there is a way out of it.

That's why I'm not looking forward to my holiday, as I can only imagine how stressful it will be. I can't see the good side of anything anymore. I would rather stay home and have a rest, and focus on becoming clean, which I have failed to achieve so far. My only hope is that being in a different environment might take my mind off painkillers. Apparently, it works for some people. Maybe it will work for me, seeing that nothing else has worked so far. In the end, I will be able to do it, because I don't have a choice. It's just something I need to do, full stop. There is no looking back.

On Friday we're finally flying to Amsterdam to see my mum. I still need to pack and get everything ready. I have the cat food, that's a start, and some cat litter, enough to last for the next three weeks. My oldest son Daniel will look after the house and the animals while four of us will be away (Larry, Flynn, Angie, and I will be going). Georgia promised to pop into the house from time to time and make sure everything's okay, and to keep an eye on the cats and the kittens.

24 AUGUST 2015

THE HOLIDAY WAS OVER IN a flash, and I didn't write while I was away. We came back from Europe on Sunday. I did really well in Europe. I managed without drugs the whole time, so that's over three weeks, four weeks actually, without codeine painkillers. What a miracle! But I've been having trouble with jet lag since our return. We had a tremendous time over there, even though things were not easy with my mum. She did her best, though, to get along with us, and I'm grateful for that. And while I was in Europe I was completely clean, four weeks altogether—the longest I've ever lasted without codeine painkillers.

It's not determination that made me stay clear of these drugs. It's because in most European countries, codeine-based painkillers can't be sold over the counter like here. I wonder why this law hasn't been introduced in Australia. So many people have died from this terrible addiction, according to the Internet. When you don't have access to your drug, it's a lot harder to abuse it. This works for people like me, who don't buy illegal stuff. I would never look for illegal drugs. It just wouldn't come to my mind, and also I would be too scared to do it. I wouldn't know where to get them from anyway. But just because I don't do illicit drugs, just because I have a roof over my head, a loving family, kids, and pets, doesn't mean I'm okay. I look okay on the outside, but on the inside it's a different story.

I didn't experience many withdrawal symptoms. We were too busy visiting the Netherlands, France, and Germany. How can you think about this stupid drug when you're on top of the Eiffel Tower? Now that I'm back at home it's a lot harder. I was okay on Monday, doing really well in spite of feeling lethargic, depressed, and without motivation, mainly due to jet lag, which is known to be worse when you fly westward like we did.

I felt sleepy but I couldn't sleep at night. I watched the shiny red numbers on my bedside table clock click by, hour after hour. Overcoming an addiction becomes a challenge as soon as you have something physically and mentally intense happening. That's when your endurance gets tested. Mine didn't last very long, unfortunately.

By Tuesday my willpower collapsed. I gave in to my urge and bought a packet of codeine painkillers, my usual brand. It was a packet of thirty because they didn't have a smaller one. This probably proves how many people abuse this drug and how the pharmaceutical industry makes a profit from it. Codeine is known to be addictive, just like other opiates, and yet you can buy it in large quantities in Australia as easily as you can buy toilet paper or jelly beans. I can't understand how this is possible, in this day and age. It's a drug, after all, just like marijuana, heroin, or ice. Perhaps I'm exaggerating, but this is my opinion.

You can walk into any chemist in Adelaide and buy codeine-based painkillers over the counter. You don't have to prove your identity, not even your age as you do with alcohol. They only ask you two or three questions: "Is it for yourself?" and "Are you on any other medication?" and sometimes "What are you using it for?" They might give you a warning that it could make you sleepy. They tell you not to take more than six tablets a day.

On drug forums, I read about people who take sixty or ninety tablets a day. And they will certainly die if they continue doing it. People get admitted to hospital with acute anaemia and life-threatening bleeding stomach ulcers. Authorities seem to turn a blind eye to this epidemic. It's a secret that no one likes to talk about, and I'm a prime example, battling this all on my own. I confessed to a doctor once, but he didn't do much to help me. He gave me a script for Valium, which was not effective with withdrawal symptoms. He wanted me to go to a drug rehabilitation place, but I don't want to be with the "real" druggies, the kind who do illegal stuff and are on the street.

I'm a fifty-year old mum and I work as an enrolled nurse. What if anyone recognises me there? Perhaps I wouldn't be able to practice as an enrolled nurse anymore. I know I have a problem, but at this stage, I can't identify myself with a junkie. I know it's not the best solution, but I will continue to follow this path on my own. It's something I have to do, because there is no real help out there. No one understands my predicament.

I only took twelve tablets out of the packet of thirty codeine painkillers. I threw the rest of the packet in the bin. I felt awful after taking these tablets, after being clean for a month. It really hit me how bad they are. At first I felt a bit euphoric, but the feeling quickly subsided, and that night I felt anxious and panicky, restless, and unable to relax. I couldn't go to sleep. My thoughts were racing. I never want to do this again. I have a strong feeling that I'm finally through with this addiction. It's been my demon, my dirty secret for too long. I don't even enjoy it anymore. It's disgusting, what it does to my mind and body.

The next day I woke up with a hangover, as though I'd drunk a bottle of vodka the night before. I felt tired, unable to focus. With my jet lag, which was still in full swing, it was a bad combination. So day one was a catastrophe, but I was determined never to do this again. I know I've said this many times before, but this is the nature of addiction. It takes time and several attempts. The secret is: Never give up, and keep trying no matter what.

Today is day two and I know it will be easier for me this time. I was clean for over four weeks prior to this, and during that time, all the codeine has been flushed out of my body. I won't have withdrawal symptoms, at least not physical side effects. I might still crave the drug mentally, but I know I can overcome this now. It's only temptation, after all.

I've overcome many temptations in my life, so this is not going to be as hard as it seems. If you think something is difficult, it will be that way. But if you think it is easy, it will be that way too. To be scared of something makes it more difficult to do. Have no fear, and it will be much easier. I will concentrate on other things and forget about my addiction. I will not label myself as an addict anymore. From now on, I'm going to be a normal person, someone who went through hell and came back as a wiser, more experienced person.

I can empathise with people who have addictions, as I'm one of them. In the past, I used to think they were weak and lacked willpower. But when the addiction takes over, there's nothing you can do about it, nothing that has to do with willpower. You can have as much willpower as you want, and it won't help you. This is because the addiction has a way to get into your mind and play with your thoughts, convincing you to take the drug "just one more time."

The addiction tells you you can control this substance, that it's not as bad as something else (like codeine is not as bad as alcohol: This has always been my excuse). You always think this is the last time and that you will give it up tomorrow. Just not today, because today, you want to take it just one more time! But you're fooling yourself, because each time you give in to it, your addiction grows stronger. *Now* is the time to give it up and to become clean, once and for all. Do it one day at a time if you want to, but *do it*, no matter what. The longer you wait, the more you're likely to die.

28 SEPTEMBER 2015

TODAY IT'S DAY SIX FOR me, and I'm doing really well. I haven't had any withdrawal symptoms at all. I feel relaxed and energetic. Sleep at night tends to elude me, especially towards the beginning of the night, but eventually I do fall asleep. I try to do some meditation, but it doesn't always work. I need to do it more seriously and regularly. My mind tends to race continuously. I tend to worry about silly things: my washing, cooking, and how much money is left in my bank account. I wish I could stop worrying so much, especially about money.

I dread going back to work because they have implemented a new computer software, and it's so complicated it gives me a headache just thinking about it. I wish I didn't hate my job. I wish I could do something I enjoy, something I can be passionate about. I would like to do something that makes use of my skills. I'd like to be creative and innovative in my job. I like people too, and I don't mind any chores, as long as I can see the meaning and the long-term effect of what I'm doing. I should have been an arts teacher. Maybe it's not too late, after all. Fifty years is only half of the average life span of a healthy person. These days, you can easily expect to live to a hundred, if you look after your health. That's the secret: looking after your health, with a good diet, regular exercise, and without drugs.

I don't mind doing repetitive tasks if it leads to something meaningful, but with nursing I can't find any sense in it anymore. The paperwork is overwhelming and has taken over everything. It has become more important than the person. You can't spend quality time with the old people anymore. Nursing homes have become factories, and every resident seems to be depressed. No wonder, if they're treated like machines, and not like individuals who have human needs and desires.

I used to love being an enrolled nurse in aged care, but now I don't feel any enthusiasm for what I do anymore. A few years ago, I tried to do be a counsellor, and I was good at it, but it wasn't a regular income because I didn't have enough clients. I did enjoy that type of work, though, and I'd like to do it again one day if possible. I would like to take responsibility for my own life. I don't want to be in denial about things anymore. I have created my own problems. I have created my addiction, and I suffer for it now.

Night shifts are detrimental for me. This is how I became addicted to codeine in the first place. And yet I haven't really done much to find another, better career path. I feel stuck in one place. I admit feeling sorry for myself. I haven't taken any real productive steps to improve my circumstances. My life is the result of my own actions. I know this, and yet reading this diary it sounds like a big complaint, like I'm constantly whinging. But I have a lot of blessings in my life, and I don't need to feel sorry for myself.

I want to stop finding excuses for what I've done to myself, for who I have become. Perhaps I've improved slightly since May, when I started this diary, but not enough. By now, I should be clean for longer than five days. On the other hand, any improvement counts, and I need to remember that no day is wasted, as long as I stay clear of codeine painkillers. They will ruin my life and kill me eventually, if I keep taking them. I don't want them in my life anymore. I want to forget this addiction, erase it from my mind and body, and concentrate on the things that matter. I want to get away from nursing and find a career that is not stressful, something that suits me better, that is rewarding and satisfying, a job that enables me to use both my creativity and people skills.

I have a lot of potential, but it has been stifled by my nursing profession, which for me has become a way to make money and pay the bills. Every self-improvement book says you should follow your passion, and not settle for anything less, if you really want to achieve happiness and success. There is no other way, and I will make it my mission to think about a new career and maybe apply for positions online, or find another way to quit nursing. I might only work one shift a week to keep my registration as an enrolled nurse.

Today I applied online for a position with the Australian Scholarship Group. I sent in my resume and will see what comes out of it. I could see myself going to people's places, having a chat, and selling them this programme that is excellent if you want to put money aside for your children's education. It's been around for many years and it's not a scam. I subscribed to it for Angie a few months ago and wished I'd done it earlier. I wish I'd done it for my other kids too. I will certainly do it for my grandchildren when they come along. It will help them towards their education. What a wonderful gift. This is the type of job I can imagine doing, something with a purpose.

Thinking about codeine painkillers, I recall how many times I've driven to a pharmacy in the last few years, buying this awful stuff that I thought kept me going. What an illusion! Drugs don't make your lives easier; on the contrary. They only pull you down, and in the end, they will destroy you and affect all the people around you. They ruin everything. And legal drugs are no better than illegal ones. I would like to campaign to make it illegal for all codeine-based painkillers to be sold over the counter.

I'd like to help others with the same addiction. I'm not the best example, and it has taken me ages to get to this point. In spite of many efforts and attempts, I'm still not sure if I've beaten my addiction for good. Only time will tell. I will be sure once I've stayed clear of codeine for at least three months without falling off the wagon. Six months would be even better. I don't crave this substance as much as I used to.

I think my trip to Europe helped me a lot. The laws there don't allow for these products to be sold without a doctor's prescription. The secret then is to be in a place where the drug is not available. If it had been available in pharmacies there, without a script, I would have bought a packet, as I was tempted to have some on a few occasions. The first time it happened, I had a bad migraine and I asked for some codeine painkillers. The pharmacist looked at me strangely and told me that in Holland, it's illegal to sell anything with codeine over the counter. I think they should implement this rule in Australia as soon as possible, or a lot of people will get addicted and suffer terrible consequences.

2 OCTOBER 2015

TODAY IS DAY TEN AND I am doing okay. The good news is that my cravings have gone. I don't want any codeine in my system anymore. I don't feel like buying a packet of codeine painkillers and swallowing twelve or more tablets at once. I'm not sure why. Probably because I was away in Europe for three weeks, not able to get hold of my drug of choice without a prescription. I was forced to stay clean. Of course I could have obtained a prescription somehow. But it would have been bothersome, and it would have raised questions. I would have had to make up a lie to obtain the script. I think I've had enough of that: lying, stealing, pretending. I don't have the energy to do it anymore.

It angers me that in this country, anyone can obtain large amounts of codeine over the counter. Why are we so backwards with our laws? Why doesn't this government do more to protect its people? Even in the media, the focus is on the "ice epidemic," but no one mentions codeine painkillers. No one knows how many people have died as a consequence of their addiction to over-the-counter medications containing codeine. Every year, hundreds of people are treated for codeine dependency, and according to the Internet, some take as many as one hundred tablets a day.

Pharmaceutical companies are happy to cash in big profits at the detriment of people like me, ordinary mums and dads. These are people who would never abuse illegal drugs and not even prescription drugs. These are people who bought this product to treat genuine pain, like a headache, toothache, or back pain. Their addiction began innocently, with a trip to the chemist and a packet of one of the most common brands of codeine painkillers.

Perhaps they had stress at work or at home, relationship problems, or maybe difficulties raising children on their own or without enough support.

Codeine smooths everything out. It makes the unbearable bearable, until everything falls apart and breaks into little pieces. It's a time bomb waiting to explode. Fatigue, irritability, and uncomfortable physical side effects begin to appear as the addiction progresses. One day you find yourself unable to carry out the simplest task without taking your drug first. It keeps you going, no matter what. And the worst thing about it is that no one notices, because it's a hidden addiction. It's a silent killer.

There are no external signs, not like with cigarettes, alcohol or other drugs. The person is in control, doesn't get drunk or stoned. There is no smell. The person continues to be productive, continues to work, continues to raise children, and does the cooking and cleaning. The only change may be fatigue, a need to sleep or nap a lot. Codeine interferes with your natural sleep patterns. It also affects your bodily functions, making you hungover the next day, as if you'd drunk too much alcohol. Despite these effects, you keep functioning. You may get headaches, but nothing you can't cope with. You just take more painkillers to treat them. Sometimes nausea can be a problem, or even vomiting. It's the body's natural reaction to get rid of toxic substances. Codeine is a poison, and it will make you sick. Ibuprofen and paracetamol (acetaminophen) are also poisons, and these substances are mixed with codeine when you buy painkillers over the counter. They can both cause a lot of damage to your internal organs.

This is the most insidious addiction of all. I want to make people aware of it and to help others with the same problem. I just heard something on the news, as Larry's television is always switched on in the bedroom next to the study. In Australia, there is talk about making over-the-counter codeine based painkillers illegal without a prescription. It will happen as of June 2016. Too many people have died from misuse of these products or overdoses. The pharmaceutical industry won't be happy, as they're selling millions of these packets every month. I hope this law will get through, as it would prevent a lot unnecessary deaths as well as damaged livers and kidneys. It will still be possible for people to obtain these drugs, but only through a physician, which more difficult, and a deterrent. Doctors will not prescribe these painkillers unless they believe people genuinely need them for chronic pain.

I was lucky to go to Europe and be away from temptation, so I could have a detox period, before heading back to Australia, where it is so freely available that they might as well sell it at the supermarket. I can only guess how many silent victims like me are out there, suffering and feeling horrible, blaming and hating themselves. But it's not really their fault. This is a highly addictive substance, and anyone can get addicted to it. It's like distributing heroin freely to everyone, and then wondering why so any people get hooked on it.

The ice epidemic might be serious, but this kind of addiction is probably more widespread and more difficult to address. They will need to ban these drugs from being sold over the counter sooner than later. I wish they would do it right away, so I won't be tempted to buy them again. I never want to feel the guilt and shame I experience after taking a lot of codeine painkiller tablets. They make me feel better and stronger for a while, but the consequences are devastating. They make me forget my weaknesses and I have a lot of energy to accomplish things for a few hours, until the effect subsides. Then I regret what I've done and wish I could go back in time. I wish I'd never taken any of those tablets. I wish I'd never bought my first packet of codeine painkillers. The euphoria they produce is a short-lived boost that leaves a bitter aftertaste.

If you have a problem with codeine painkillers, please talk to someone. Don't be like me and stay in the dark. Come out of your shell, confide in someone. Tell your partner, your family. At least I talked to a doctor about it. He made me do a blood test, and it showed that my liver was beginning to be damaged by this drug. It frightened me and it was like a wake-up call for me. Talking to someone about it will perhaps make your addiction appear *real* for the first time. It will make you realise that it is a serious problem, and that you need all the help and support you can get.

When you keep things to yourself, you can easily deny that you have a problem. Tell your loved ones about it. They will understand. I don't know why I still can't bring myself to open up to my husband and children (at least the older ones). I'm so ashamed and feel that I'm letting them down, but that's absurd. It would be better to tell them the truth. I've always wanted to be strong for them, to be some kind of role model. But what I'm teaching them by remaining silent is to hide your problems inside yourself, instead of opening up about them. I wish I could be open about my addiction.

Exercise helps a lot, as it stimulates your body's endorphins. It will make you feel better, mentally and physically. Go for a walk, a jog, a swim, do some yoga or some housework. It takes your mind off the drug when you focus on a task. Take it easy. Take it a day at a time, without worrying how you will cope tomorrow. Tomorrow is another day. Distract yourself, watch some TV, your favourite movies or series on DVD. Read books that are page-turners like thrillers or crime novels, or anything that keeps you involved. Avoid stressful situations, and don't take on too many responsibilities. If your job is too stressful, think about a change of career. This is what I want to do.

I have to go back to work tonight, and while I'm dreading it, I also know that I can get out of this industry if I really want to. There are other ways to make money, to pay the bills. I'm sure I will be able to do it eventually. I want to help other people. I want to help children and teenagers. I want my life to make sense, to have a purpose. I know this would take away my anxiety, knowing that I can make a difference. I want to tell people that I've been to hell and back. If I can quit this drug, they can too. My addiction was so powerful that it took over everything. I could not go for more than a few days without driving to the chemist and buying a packet of codeine painkillers.

My mental cravings seem to have disappeared, but I still experience physical withdrawal symptoms, like diarrhea, stomach cramps, lots of yawning, constant fatigue, low energy, depression, low motivation, sneezing, and aches and pains all over my body. It's getting less and less, though, with symptoms taking turns. One day I might experience a lot of fatigue, depression, and yawning for instance. The next day it's stomach pains and diarrhea. The next it's back and shoulder pain. It's like the symptoms are going round and round as the drug progressively leaves my body.

I never want to go back to it. I don't care how long these symptoms last. I can put up with them. I can still take ibuprofen or paracetamol, but without the codeine in it. I try not to put any chemicals into my body. I stick to herbal remedies like St John's wort for depression and Valerian for sleeplessness. Insomnia is another side effect of codeine withdrawal.

The most important is not to give up, even if you relapse numerous times. Never stop trying. You will succeed eventually. Maybe go to a hospital or rehab centre, so they can lock you away and you don't have access to this drug. As soon as you stop taking it, you'll begin to feel better. The first few days are the hardest. Then you'll begin to heal. Your body will soon recover, your liver and kidneys will start working properly again. Soon you'll be able to sleep better, think clearly, and make rational decisions.

3 OCTOBER 2015

Today is day eleven, and I was at work last night! I did really well. I wasn't tempted to buy codeine painkillers from the chemist before I went to work, and I wasn't tempted to look in the pharmacy box. I feel like a different person. I feel *normal*. My brain is not playing games with me anymore. I still lack energy and motivation, but I do everything I can to overcome my lethargy. Physically, I don't seem to have any withdrawal symptoms anymore, just a queasy stomach, but that could be due to anxiety. I can't blame everything on withdrawal. The pains in my body have subsided. I just have some back and shoulder pain, but this is nothing new. I need to do more exercise, more swimming, and yoga. Unfortunately, I can't fit it into my schedule when I work night shifts. Another three nights to go and it will be over. I feel more balanced emotionally. When Larry says something I don't like, I don't feel the need to retaliate or justify myself. I just let it go, which feels like a relief.

What I don't like is that my appetite has come back with a vengeance. I hardly used to eat anything when I was on codeine. Now I can't stop being hungry. I want to eat all the time. I'm putting on weight, which is a nuisance. Controlling my appetite is a problem, but I won't let it affect me. I'd rather put on some weight than die. I simply can't face being a codeine addict for another ten years. Just the thought makes me sick. I don't want to be an old junkie lady, on her way to an early grave, leaving her loved ones behind. I have a good relationship with my kids, and I don't want to jeopardize it. I want to be there for them when they need me.

According to Internet sources, codeine is extremely addictive, and it's one of the hardest drugs to detox from. I can believe it—I am sure it's as addictive as heroin. But it's more cunning too, especially in Australia and in the UK, where it is sold over the counter, which makes it seem so innocuous. I don't know if there are any other countries that sell codeine so easily to the public. It's a crime, but I can't keep getting upset about it. After all, some people use it for genuine pain and at the recommended dosage.

Not everyone who takes codeine painkillers has addiction problems and abuses these drugs. But I'm sure the number of people who do is quite frightening. These products are sold in combination with paracetamol (acetaminophen) and ibuprofen, which doesn't make them innocuous—quite the contrary. These components do a lot of damage to the body: Paracetamol is bad for your liver and ibuprofen destroys your kidneys.

Maybe it would be better if they sold codeine on its own, without these additives. It is possible to do the cold water extraction, but I tried it and it's not satisfying. It's also a hassle and not easy to hide from your family, not like popping a few tablets out of a packet that looks harmless to observers. "I have a terrible migraine and this is the only medication that helps." It's easy to justify yourself to others.

I think codeine painkiller addicts are a special breed of people. We may be junkies, but we would never do illegal drugs. Some of us might not even drink alcohol or smoke cigarettes. We wouldn't do marijuana or ice. We wouldn't smoke drugs or inject them. We don't have druggie friends or dealers. Our dealer is the chemist, or several chemists if we do the "pharmacy round" to avoid raising suspicion. We are ordinary, normal people. We minimise our addiction and make it look less destructive than it is. We think popping tablets we can buy without a script makes our addiction safe. After all, if this was dangerous stuff, it wouldn't be sold freely. There would be some restrictions, at least.

It's a big decision to give up a drug that controls every aspect of your life. You need to ask yourself *how* you will deal with every day stresses. How will you cope with your emotions, your disappointments? What will you do when things are out of control, when the bills pile up, the kids fight, and your partner is uncooperative? You need to be prepared for the worst, while keeping a positive mindset. You can hope for the best while being prepared for any eventuality.

Nothing is as bad as killing yourself slowly with this drug. There is a solution to every problem, but only if you don't give in to your addiction, only if you remain clean and clear-headed. If you keep taking painkillers, you will slowly spiral downwards, no matter how much energy you put into your career, your relationships, your home. You will drown.

One day you'll find yourself in bed, feeling sick, maybe vomiting, unable to get up. You might even die.

Is it best to go cold turkey or to taper down your intake? I don't know. Different things work for different people. We're not all the same. According to Internet sources, the success rate is better with cold turkey. Personally I would find it difficult to reduce my intake progressively. As soon as I have some codeine in my system, I want more of it, just to make the nice feeling of calm energy last longer.

I had to do it cold turkey. There was no other way for me. But I had a lot of relapses too, and that's fine. I think that's normal with a highly addictive substance. At least I didn't have to go to rehab. But I would advise anyone to go to rehab if they have this problem, and if they think it might help. It's too hard to do it on your own. This drug is so easily available that you'll never quit your addiction unless you're locked up for three or four weeks, maybe even six weeks. It's so important to be away from this drug, so you can become a normal person again.

7 OCTOBER 2015

I FEEL TERRIBLE. NOT ONLY disappointed in myself, but sick. My head is pounding and I'm feeling nauseous. I don't know what to do anymore. I relapsed on Monday night. I could blame it on work, but I won't. Work, especially night shift, is just an excuse, like everything else. I'm in agony today, after what I've done.

I can't take codeine painkillers anymore, or I end up with the worst migraine. I don't have much love for myself at the moment. I can't stand myself, what I do to myself, the way I pretend to be in control, when in reality, I am a mess. I don't want to die, because I want to be there for others, but I feel helpless when it comes to looking after myself. I don't take proper care of my body. I don't know why I can't be normal, like everyone else. No one else I know has this problem.

It all started on Sunday, after work. I had a couple of oxazepam tablets in my pocket (oxazepam is a short-acting benzodiazepine, used for the treatment of anxiety). I wanted to take these tablets to help me sleep better after my night shift. It's often difficult to go to sleep after a night shift, and I justified my desire for the drugs this way. In reality

I was on a downwards slope. I fell asleep after I took the tablets, but when I woke up I felt groggy and uncomfortable. My mind was in a fog, and I couldn't think straight. I felt awkward and slightly depressed.

I didn't feel like going back to work, even though it was my last shift and I could have just got it over and done with. Instead I preferred to dwell on it. I felt discouraged. Suddenly I felt the urge to take some codeine painkiller tablets. I needed these tablets to cope with one more night shift I had to do. I usually work four nights in a row, and the last night is the worst. I need the money, though, and I don't have a choice. I have to do these nights, but I don't have to take codeine painkiller tablets, knowing they will make me feel worse.

I took twelve tablets, which is not as much as I'd normally take. In the past I would take up to twenty-four tablets, which is twice as much. But I'm not used to this drug anymore. It gave me a bit of a boost, and I arrived at work feeling energetic. It didn't last long though, and I soon crashed. My energy levels quickly fell and towards the morning, after my break, I felt really tired and worn out. I felt I couldn't cope with the rest of my shift. I went to the pharmacy box and found some tramadol, three tablets altogether, in a blister pack that was due to go back to the pharmacy, as the person had passed away. I took these tablets and discarded the packet, hiding it under a heap of papers in the bin, so nobody would find it.

I took the tablets and immediately felt better, but only for a short while. When I got home, I was emotional and tearful, and tired. I had to drive my daughter to a horse-riding day camp and nearly had an accident on the way. I couldn't focus properly. I made irrational decisions, nearly colliding with a truck. I decided to be more careful. My guardian angel was looking after us, for sure. I can only thank God for not ending up in an accident involving my precious daughter Angie. It's a scary thought, and another reason to give up this insanity.

I spent most of the day in bed trying to sleep, but I was restless and anxious. I did some cooking in the afternoon. Then I went to pick up Angie from her camp. She was tired and didn't seem happy, even though she'd had a full day. Sometimes I wonder if it's worth spending the money to do things like that. She ends up with the idea that she wants a horse, but it's not something I can afford right now.

I want Angie to be happy, but I also want to stay alive. This is my priority now, and I will do everything I can to achieve this. I might have to hand in my notice and find a different job, or go back to the agency. I only want to work a couple of nights a week. Maybe doing four nights in a row is my downfall, and I should not do it anymore, if I really want to stay away from painkillers.

My head is still pounding now, and I wish I could go back in time and change everything I've done so far. I made some bad choices and put a lot of poison into my body. How can I get better? How can I heal once and for all? I know my liver can regenerate itself if I give it a chance, and this is what I want to do. I don't just want to try, but really do it. *Trying* implies failure, so I will simply say that I will do it, no matter what. I've done well so far, despite my relapses: only two since I came back from Europe. That's not the end of the world. And the reason why I feel so sick is because I'm actually getting better. My body is not used to this poison anymore, so it affects me more.

Now codeine gives me a rebound headache, which is a good thing, as it tells me not to take it anymore. I never want to be in that much pain again, and this is a decision I can make for myself. The after-effect is too devastating. It's like the worst hangover. This is why I stopped drinking alcohol some years ago. I had a horrible hangover once and I said to myself: never again. I haven't drunk since. I can do the same for codeine painkillers.

I hate what codeine painkillers do to me, how I feel the next day after a binge. It really puts me off. I want to become clean, but I don't want to count the days anymore: day one, two, three, four, five. What for? It's just another way to set myself up for failure. Once the decision is made, counting becomes unnecessary. I will just keep recording my progress in this diary until I'm a hundred percent sure I'm healed, once and for all. I knew this was the case with alcohol when I gave it up, and it wasn't a big deal. It just happened, and I knew I would never have a drink again. It was a simple decision. I want the same to happen to me now with codeine-based painkillers. I'm done with them. I don't want to suffer anymore.

22 OCTOBER 2015

NO MORE FALLING OFF THE wagon! I'm doing well. I was reading a motivational book the other day, and it talked a lot about goal setting. It says you should write down your goals, and you will be much more likely to achieve them. I can't remember the percentage of success compared to those who don't write down their goals, but it was impressive. It also said to be specific, to give a time and date and precisely what you want to achieve.

For instance, if you want to lose weight, you should write: "I will weigh ... kilos on the (day) of (months) 20 ... (year), at (time) exactly." I decided my liver tests would return to normal on the fifteenth of December 2015. I now avoid all medications, not just codeine-based painkillers. I stay clear of simple ibuprofen and paracetamol too. I tend to take too many of those. I've also decided to change my diet. I eat more fruit and vegetables and avoid sugar and processed foods. I drink mainly water. I started making my own coconut yoghourt. When I crave sugar, I sprinkle some stevia powder over my yoghourt or add some to my tea.

My health is my wealth. I need to do everything in my power to regain it. My body tends to heal quickly, and

I can already sense it repairing itself. The body is such a marvellous machine. You can abuse it for years, but give it a chance and it bounces back to normal. The body always works hard at maintaining a balance of good health and wellbeing. We just need to give it the tools and leave it alone, not interfere with drugs or other chemicals.

I decided to join the gym. I want to become an "exercise addict," to replace one addiction with another one. At least exercise will be good for me. And it helps the body to produce endorphins. I will feel calmer and won't have any cravings. I feel so much better already. My mind is clearer, I can focus better. Even my piano playing has improved, and my memory is better.

I quit my job because it was making me relapse. I couldn't handle it anymore. I worry about money, but I joined an agency and I'm happier doing casual jobs. It suits me better. I dislike the boredom of staying in a permanent job. I lose my motivation. Now I do different things, I go to different places, and I have some variety. But the shifts haven't been coming in too frequently. I will not panic though, and I will remain patient. There will be shifts in the end, especially with Christmas just around the corner.

Overall I'm a happier person already. I'm glad about the goal I set myself. I know my liver is capable of healing 100 percent, if only I give it a chance, which is what I'm doing right now. I pray that I'll remain on this track, headed in the right direction. I don't want to go backwards. I don't want to count the days anymore, just live a day at a time, and deal with issues as they arise. I can't solve all my problems at once.

23 OCTOBER 2015

YESTERDAY I THOUGHT I WAS doing so well, but I was wrong. I need to be careful. I need to be on my guard all the time or the addiction will start talking to me, and it will tell me to take this horrible drug again. I can't understand myself sometimes. Why is it that I want something, but then I act against my own will? Why are we humans so fallible? Or is it just me? I don't know. I wish I could be strong all the time, like these people you read about in books or magazines. Or maybe they hide the truth about themselves, too?

I hate how society wants women to be thin all the time, even when they've had kids. Women over fifty have to be mutton dressed up as lamb. I can't stand this kind of pressure, but I can't help giving in to it. I'm always trying to lose weight. It's one of my weaknesses, but it never got me anywhere. Even though my BMI is normal, it's not good enough for me. I want to be skinnier. It's an obsession.

Since last weak, I cut sugar and carbohydrates out of my diet, after reading one of those "quit sugar" books. The result: I put on two kilos. I couldn't believe my eyes when I saw the numbers on the scale. I felt dreadful yesterday.

I had no energy, and I felt really low, almost suicidal. I saw no solution to my problems: my addiction to codeine, my work issues, having to do night shifts, Flynns's private school fees, and the cost of Angie's extra-curricular activities (gymnastics, piano, horse-riding). I don't want them to miss out, but I struggle financially.

Maybe I should relax, be more laid-back, and use my credit card. Maybe I shouldn't worry about the bills. Larry and I have an arrangement: We share the bills, including the mortgage, and he puts some money into my account every week for Angie, our only common child. During our holiday overseas, Larry was generous, often paying for meals and accommodation. But back home he reverted to his usual stingy self. He is tight with his money and doesn't help me with the expenses for my children from my marriage to Brett. He says it's not his problem. He's right, but I wish he would help me more.

I need to keep working, but every time I do, I put myself at risk of using painkillers. I'm getting better at resisting temptation, though. On Monday, I worked in a busy and stressful place, but I remained firm in my resolve not to take any tablets. I focused on my work, that's all. No excuses, no escape. It felt good being strong, and in the morning I was proud of myself. Even though I was tired, I felt better in my body and my mind. I was more focused and had more clarity than usual after a night shift.

I still can't understand what happened yesterday but I need to get to the bottom of it, even though I hate admitting that I did it again. It wasn't as bad as before. I only took six tablets of codeine painkillers. It really affected me, as I hadn't taken any for a long time. I went straight to bed and slept like a log, but woke in the morning with a headache. I took some ibuprofen without codeine. I felt normal again later on that morning, although a bit tired. I decided to stop worrying and take things as they come.

I worry that I might not get enough shifts with the agency. I have a couple of thousand dollars put aside, so I should be all right, even if I don't get any work for a week or two. I just need to be patient and relax. I can use my time to go to the gym if I don't have any work. I need to concentrate on improving my health. This is what I can do, instead of telling myself that the only way out is to kill myself. I know it's senseless, but this is what happens in my head. Sometimes I just feel powerless over my negative thoughts, no matter how much positive thinking I force myself to do.

My wisdom tooth is giving me trouble. I will have to get it taken out on Wednesday and this really worries me, as I don't want to use too many painkillers. Maybe I will only take them for a day. My body heals quickly. Even though the dentist says I won't be able to work for a week, I'm sure I'll be back on track in a couple of days. I bounce back easily from things like that. I had three wisdom teeth taken out in the past, one after the other. The only one that caused me trouble was infected and the infection lasted for two weeks after the extraction. I was in agony. I never took strong painkillers though, only paracetamol, as I was breastfeeding Georgia at the time. It was a long time ago. I wish I could go back to those days, when I had no knowledge of codeine-based painkillers and their effect.

I would give anything to be able to press a "reset" button in my brain and delete everything, start anew. Maybe this is what I need to do in my mind, my imagination. Press the reset button. I can just take plain ibuprofen without codeine after my wisdom tooth extraction. It's up to me. I don't want to abuse myself anymore, as I'm getting better. I'm getting over my addiction. I wouldn't swallow thirty codeine painkiller tablets in a single day anymore. I wouldn't swallow twenty-four, and not even twelve. I can't do this to myself anymore.

I believe my liver *is* recovering and will be completely healed by the fifteenth of December. I have written it down as my most important goal in life. If I don't trust myself, I trust God that He will help me with this. I'm not particularly religious, but I believe there is a God and that He is there for us, even if we don't notice it. I will ask Him for help; it can't do any harm.

I've let myself down, but I can pick myself up and start again. It's never too late. I will overcome this, no matter what. I don't want to die.

2 NOVEMBER 2015

IT's BEEN TEN DAYS SINCE I last wrote in this diary. I can't believe it. I am so ashamed! I have relapsed numerous times. I had my wisdom tooth extracted on Wednesday, almost a week ago now, and for five days in a row I took massive amounts of codeine painkillers. The pain was atrocious. I've never been in such agony. This is the worst depression I've ever experienced, as it is physical and mental at the same time.

I feel a bit better today, for the first time since the wisdom tooth operation, which was done under "twilight" anaesthetic. Now I have to start all over again. Today is day one. I'll have to count the days again until I'm out of the woods. I never want to take these horrible painkillers again. I feel like a zombie, like a shadow of myself. I want to be *myself* again, a real person, with real feelings and emotions, not just some sort of robot. I don't want to be suicidal anymore. I want to enjoy life, make the most out of it. Why is it so difficult for me to achieve this simple goal?

I won't give up. This is *my* life, my chance to be happy and healthy. I won't throw it away. Even if I don't live to a hundred, I still want a good life span, and at least reach the age of eighty. I would like to live longer, as long as I'm fit and can do yoga. I don't want to be one of these old people needing a walking stick, shuffling from side to side and falling over because they've lost their muscle strength, coordination, and balance. I want to be an example, an inspiration to others. This is what I've always wanted to do, but it has eluded me so far.

Health is the most important thing. To me it means everything, and yet I can't get a grip on it, I can't control what I do, direct my thoughts and actions. I want to eat a healthy diet, and I haven't decided yet whether I want to be vegan or not. Doing yoga almost implies being a vegan, for some reason. They say it gives you more flexibility. I don't know if it's true. At least, I want to be a vegetarian and eat wholesome foods, like fruit and vegetables and beans.

This is my last hurdle, this wisdom tooth. I got the other ones extracted years ago. Why did I leave this one for so long? I never had the time and money to have it extracted. But lately, it started showing signs of infection. I could feel pain radiating in my jaw. I decided to do something about it before it got worse.

But after the operation I went on a codeine painkiller binge for five days in a row. I don't need to be exact about the number of tablets I took, but the count was between twenty and thirty a day. I feel so ashamed and so bad about myself, which doesn't help. I have decided to recover, to start all over. Today the pain is bearable. My jaw is not so swollen. I can feel it healing, the gap where my tooth used to be. I wish my soul would heal too. I wish I could let go of all pain and tension and just be myself.

Addictions don't arise out of the blue. There is always a reason why we turn to a substance to numb ourselves. In my case, it's definitely *insecurity*. I feel I have a lot of financial insecurity. I'm always scared I won't have enough money. But it started out as emotional insecurity. This was a big thing, especially at the beginning of my relationship with Larry. I didn't trust him, especially after what my first husband Brett did to me. He cheated on me and eventually walked out on me.

I didn't believe Larry really loved me. I expected things to go wrong, to come to an end. I had separation anxiety. I was sure he would dump me and I would be left on my own again. I'm terrified of being alone, which is one of my problems. But I know I'm not crazy. There is a lot of health in me too, and I do have willpower and determination. I just need to use them in my life. I need to keep doing what I've decided to do, and not stop, not fall off the wagon. My objective remains that my liver test will come back normal on the fifteenth of December of this year. I know I still have time to achieve this goal. It only takes four weeks for the liver to fully regenerate itself.

Today I will go back to bed, as I have no energy left. I want my jaw to heal completely so I can put this thing behind me and forget about my relapse. It was pretty bad, but beating myself up won't make it better. I will only feel more guilty and miserable, which will lead to another relapse. This is my last chance, and I can do it.

There is no need to take these tablets anymore. The pain will soon be completely gone, and I will feel better. My body has the ability to regenerate itself quickly. It's a wonderful machine. If I can stop putting so much pressure on myself and just let it happen, then I will heal. Today is day one, and I will start counting the days again, at least until the fifteenth of December.

16 NOVEMBER 2015

I'VE BEEN STRUGGLING SINCE MAY to get rid of this addiction, and I'm still in the same boat today. I did night shifts on Wednesday, Thursday, and Friday, and on the weekend I really went overboard and took sixty codeine painkiller tablets within twenty-four hours. I felt awful. I don't know why I did it. Was it frustration, depression, discouragement that my situation is not improving? I don't know.

I was doing fairly well before my wisdom tooth extraction, but then I became weak and now I'm back to square one. Today is day two and I will count the days again, even though it depresses me. I've relapsed so many times. Sometimes I just want to end it and kill myself, because I feel there is no solution to my dilemma. My goal of being healthy seems to elude me. I want to do everything I can to achieve it, but it doesn't work. I am caught in some sort of web, struggling to free myself, only to get caught in another web and then another. There seems to be no end to it, and I'm on the verge of giving up.

The only thing that stops me is my beautiful little girl Angie. I don't want to leave her without a mum. She loves me so much, and yet she doesn't know what sort of person

I really am. Behind my façade, there is self-destruction, addiction, lying, and stealing. People think I'm doing well, but in reality I'm like a sinking ship, the *Titanic*. God, please help me, I can't live like this. I would give anything to be clean and stop craving painkillers. As soon as the stress accumulates in my life, I turn to them like a crutch, but it's a fatal crutch. Why can't I get addicted to something that's good for me? At least this morning I went to the gym and I feel a bit better. I still don't have any energy, and when I got home I had to nap for three hours.

On Saturday I finally spoke to Larry about my addiction. It was the hardest thing I've ever done. It took me a long time, and a lot of thinking. At first he didn't want to hear about my problem, but then I reassured him it had nothing to do with him. I told him I became addicted to painkillers. I told him I had managed to stop for a while, until my wisdom tooth started giving me trouble and needed to be extracted. I was in tears, and he was very understanding. He told me it could be due to depression, which is true. I think he also suspects it has something to do with him, with his attitude towards me. He can be uncaring and cold-hearted towards me at times. Maybe he will start changing and show a bit more compassion towards me now.

I don't know if I want to stay with him forever. I want to get better first, and then I will make up my mind. I do love him, but he doesn't do much for me or for the house. The house is falling to pieces and he doesn't want to do anything about it. When I mention any repairs that need to be done, he gets angry. I just have to accept things as they are and ignore that our home is deteriorating, almost in a state of disrepair. Of course I can't blame it all on Larry; it's my responsibility too, to look after it. But without money and without the skills, it's impossible. I'm not a handy person, and I can't fix it on my own.

I wish we could do things together like a normal couple, but in a way I've given up and don't care about anything. I just don't want to die. I'm not ready to leave this planet yet. I still feel that I have a lot of things to do. I want to be there for my kids. Who else have they got? My ex Brett isn't of much help. He has psychological problems and escapes from them with alcohol. He turns into a different person when he's under the influence. He becomes unreliable and neglects his responsibilities. I would be worried if Flynn had to live with him.

I have no choice. I need to keep going, even if it's hard, and even if it seems impossible. My goal is still for my liver test to come back clean on the fifteenth of December. I pray that it will, and that I'll be able to stay clean until then. I pray that my liver will regenerate itself.

19 NOVEMBER 2015

DAY FIVE TODAY, AND I'M hanging in there, but only by a thread. I need to use a lot of willpower to stay on track, but so far it hasn't been too bad and I haven't had too many thoughts of temptation, although the desire for my drug of choice is still strong. Maybe it will stay like that forever, something I will have to accept, whether I like it or not. Usually day five is the worst, but today I don't feel any withdrawal symptoms or any cravings. But I feel a bit discouraged, on the verge of depression. Nothing seems to work out the way I intend it. Money is always scarce. I haven't been able to work much due to my wisdom tooth. And work is a mine field for me, a danger zone. But I have to do it.

I have to go to work to provide for my children. The problem is that I always feel like I'm living on the poverty line, no matter what. Maybe I don't work enough, but when I work more I feel more tempted to take codeine painkillers. They always lurk on the horizon, luring me back to my addiction like an index finger beckoning me to come closer and take these damn tablets, regardless of the consequences. The talk in my head convinces me that this time, I can control my intake and stick to eight tablets a day (which is still over the recommended daily amount of six, but better than twenty-four or thirty).

I need to be strong this time. No giving in, no allowing this kind of "head talk" to take over. When the addiction's talking, it's always lying. Never believe what is says for one second. It never tells you the truth. The addiction is destructive. Tell it to go away, tell it to go to hell. Once you start listening to it, you've lost the battle. You're in its grips again and it can do with you what it wants. Don't be fooled. Be alert, and don't let your guards down. This is how I have to live from now on, or I'll be back to square one in no time.

I'm quite happy with myself, though. This week I went to the gym every day. On Monday I did some cardio on the stationary bike and weights. On Tuesday I did yoga. On Wednesday I did cardio, weights, and swimming. Today I did another yoga class. The exercise really helps, and I'd advise anyone with an addiction problem to turn to it. The endorphins fill a void and make you feel better. It also takes your mind off your problems and you're less tempted to feel sorry for yourself and fall into the trap of self-medicating for not feeling right, for being depressed and without motivation.

When I take codeine painkiller tablets, I feel more energetic and motivated. I have an inner calm that nothing can affect. But I can't go on like that anymore, because I hate the after-effects of the drug, the feelings of guilt and desperation, the knowledge that I'm destroying my organs. I want my liver to heal. I want my body and mind to function properly. I don't want to die a premature death due to liver or kidney failure. I don't want to do this damage to myself anymore.

The body is a temple of the soul, and I want to respect it and look after as well as I can, with a healthy diet, exercise, rest, and sleep. Doing night shifts is a health hazard, but if I'm sensible, I can prevent it from affecting me. Staying clear of drugs is the first step. One good thing is that I drink a lot of water. Maybe that's why my kidneys haven't been damaged by the high doses of painkillers I've taken.

25 NOVEMBER 2015

I'M BACK TO SQUARE ONE, and I'm not happy about it. I didn't want to write this in my diary, but I can't pretend it hasn't happened. It would be dishonest, and by doing so my diary wouldn't serve any purpose but it would be a lie. I don't want to be that way, as there are already enough lies in my life. Yesterday my daughter Georgia had all her wisdom teeth removed. I was with her and as we left the dental surgery, I was handed a little plastic zip bag for her. It had all sorts of things in it, gauze, antibiotics, cortisone tablets for the swelling, a list of things to do and not to do, and a packet of strong codeine painkillers.

It was the end of my resolve. I was tempted. There were twenty tablets in the packet. I took the packet, left a sleeve of ten tablets in it, and I kept the rest for myself. I know it's really bad, because these painkillers were meant to be for my daughter, but at that moment I didn't care. I only thought of myself. I was feeling really good yesterday, and there was no need for me to take these painkillers, but just because they were available, I decided to take them. Normally you need a script for those, since they have double the codeine in them compared to over-the-counter tablets. This is how the addicted mind works, and it is totally irrational, because it wasn't my intention to relapse. But I felt compelled to do it.

I immediately took four tablets. You're only supposed to take two at a time, at four hour interval, as they have paracetamol in them. It didn't make me feel good. It made me feel tired and depressed. It didn't give me the kick it usually does, and the feeling of euphoria and happiness, the feeling that everything is okay. I took the rest of the packet as the afternoon progressed and felt increasingly worse, but I didn't care.

Larry came home from work in an argumentative mood. I was too lethargic to react. Nothing could touch me, which was good since I didn't argue back. Sometimes I feel like giving up my life, my marriage. It's depressing, when I think what a fantastic relationship we could have if only Larry would put more effort into it. I know he's not the only one to blame, and I have a lot of shortcomings too, but this is how I feel. My life could be so much better.

I can't blame anyone but myself for my problems. The addiction fooled me into thinking I would feel better and be able to cope better if I took painkillers. But I realise that it's an illusion. It actually makes me feel worse. I felt rotten yesterday, and I never want to experience that again. I want my body to be healthy again so I can have more energy, and a clear mind. Painkillers won't help me achieve this. They will only pull me down.

I thought that negative motivation was more powerful than positive motivation, but I was wrong. Positive motivation wins, because in the end fear can't produce lasting changes. I'm scared of liver damage and I'm scared to die, but it hasn't given me the courage to change so far. But realising that a healthy me will feel so much better and happier and will have the energy and drive to achieve my goals—this is empowering. It inspires me to change and to adopt the lifestyle I've always dreamt of. The image of perfect health was always there for me, but it was an unattainable ideal.

Today I know I can do it. I don't have to be perfect with my diet, but I can stay away from over-the-counter and prescription drugs. I can stay clean without craving the painkillers all the time. Craving only comes from the fact that I haven't made up my mind properly. Once I decide to give up codeine painkillers once and for all, without regrets and without looking back, I won't be drawn to this drug anymore. I did it with cigarettes and alcohol, so I can do it with codeine. It's a process that happens in the mind, a process of understanding that the effects of the drug are so bad that it's not worth taking it

The addiction creates the addiction, because withdrawal happens when you stop taking a substance, so your body and mind want it more. But this only occurs because you've been taking this drug for a while and you've become dependent on it. It's a vicious cycle, and the sooner you break free from it, the better, no matter what it takes. Once you've lived without the drug, you will feel normal, and you will feel much better than on any of the days you took the drug.

1 DECEMBER 2015

YESTERDAY EVERYTHING WENT WRONG AND I relapsed again. I took twenty tablets of codeine painkillers in one day. I need to surrender to things instead of panicking and resorting to drugs. Sometimes I feel so powerless that I can't cope with anything. I was worried about work. Yesterday I decided to start completing some online courses so I could enrol with a new agency.

I want to start something new, with a new attitude, and without chemical crutches. Ideally, I would like it to be something other than nursing, but for the time being, I seem to be stuck with this profession. But the truth is that I don't want to steal anymore. I don't want to take medications from my work place. I feel so ashamed about it that I can't look at my reflection in the mirror. I loathe the person I see there, and if I try to say "I love you" to myself it sounds conceited. It sounds like a lie, and I don't want to live a life of lies anymore.

I won't make promises anymore. No more resolutions, no more trying. The harder I try, the more I seem to fail. This is pathetic, and I feel like banging my head against a wall. My own ideal of living a healthy, drug-free life is all

I want. It means everything to me, and yet it constantly eludes me. It seems to be out of reach for me, and it makes me want to cry. I can't stand it anymore. I can't stand myself anymore.

I was really stressed out about these courses yesterday, and the only way I could deal with it was to get a packet of codeine painkillers from the chemist. I took ten in the morning, then another twelve in the afternoon. I threw two in the bin, as the packet had twenty-four tablets in it. It made me feel in control to throw these last two in the bin. I should have thrown the whole packet in the bin. I felt so tired afterwards and struggled to complete only one course, when I have six to do.

Today I feel terrible, very low and depressed. It's three o'clock in the afternoon, and I haven't started any more courses yet. I'm going to look at the manual handling one, as it seems to be the easiest. I'm so scared of maths and calculations. My mind can't concentrate on figures. How I am going to do this, I don't know. I will take my time and probably Google a lot of stuff. I could ask Larry for help, but I don't like the way he explains things. I'd rather do it myself, even though I'm going to be stressed again. But this time I won't take any painkillers.

I want to sort out my working situation, but I can't go back to night shifts unless I'm clean. I can't risk giving in to this addiction anymore, because I will get caught stealing medications. Eventually, I will kill myself with these drugs. Sometimes I don't understand why I cling to life, but this is what humans do, I guess. Most of us would rather live than die. It's the way we're programmed. I also have responsibilities. I have my children, especially Angie. I have to stay alive, but I won't be a super-mum anymore. I will take some time off work, and use up the last of my savings if I need to. This is something I have to do. I don't have a choice anymore. I will end up broke and Christmas will be meagre, but my health comes first. I need to put myself first, for once in my life, or I will end up in a coffin.

Today I will at least complete one course. Even if I just do one course a day, I will reach the end of this series. I will also have to do a practical refresher course, but thankfully I've already enrolled for one. I want to do this. I want a new start. With this new agency, I will have excellent work morals and a really good attitude. I will put 100 percent in my work. It's not what I really wish to do, and it's not what makes me happy, as it is still nursing. But I can pretend to like it, at least for a while. I will feel better if I don't fight against it, if I accept it.

Nursing is not a fulfilling job for me anymore, but unfortunately I ended up in this profession, and at the moment I can't do much else until my situation changes. Getting rid of my addiction is the most important thing for me. The rest will follow, and my life will improve. This is the only goal I have at the moment, and I need to put 110 percent into it, unless I want to continue this way, which is not an option.

Why are addictions so hard to break? In my case, insecurity, worry, and fear play a big role. With codeine painkillers I feel stronger, in control, and free of anxiety. I have more courage. I feel that I can cope with anything. When I don't take it, I feel weak and depressed. I often feel there is no way out. I've tried so many strategies to get away from night shifts, but nothing seems to make a difference. I continue to be unsuccessful. Sometimes I feel my life is out of control.

Perhaps the addiction is some kind of distraction for me, a way to immediately get rid of feelings I don't want to feel. But a chemical solution is not a *real* solution. It's just a Band-Aid, and it never lasts. In the end, it only makes things worse. This is what I need to realise and keep in mind. It will never make things better. It always brings more problems with it. Now I feel so tired that I can cope even less with my life, with all the different chores I need to do. It's a vicious cycle, and the sooner I get out of it, the better.

I did really well when I was in Europe because I had no access to this drug. But here in Australia, I have to start all over again. God, how I wish they would ban over-the-counter codeine painkillers! The sooner they do it, the better. But the greedy pharmaceutical industry doesn't want to miss out on its millions or billions. I guess these are their bestselling products, and taking them away would deprive a lot of people of money and jobs. In the meantime, it's depriving a lot of people of their lives.

7 DECEMBER 2015

I WASN'T GOING TO WRITE in my diary but I promised that I would be 100 percent honest, so I can't avoid it. The weekend was really bad and I feel like I'm hitting rock bottom. I won't even talk about it. I think I've reached the end of my tether. It feels like when I gave up alcohol. From that day on, I knew I would never drink again, and that was it. There was no struggle, no questioning my decision. I've never looked back since. I've never regretted making that decision; on the contrary, I've always known I can enjoy myself without alcohol, so I really don't need it. Now I've reached the same point with codeine painkillers. I can cope without it, even when I'm at work. Actually, I know I can cope better *without* codeine in my system. It takes my energy away. My life would be so much better without that poison in my body.

All these years, I've made it hard for myself: to work, to enjoy myself, to save money. Half the time I can't work and I have to refuse shifts because I've been taking too many of these tablets. For instance, I could have worked last night but had to refuse because I took a lot of codeine painkillers over the weekend and I felt awful. I wasn't going to write this, but I promised to tell the truth without trying to make it sound better than it is. I will never get better with these drugs, and the only thing I can do is to *stop*. I can't continue that way anymore.

At the root of my addiction is *insecurity*. Not only regarding money, but regarding my relationship with my husband. I had a fight with Larry and slept in another room on Saturday night. I found that he was not spending enough quality time with me and not taking any initiative with outings. I told him it's always *me* who has to plan everything, whether we go to the restaurant or on holidays. After that he changed his attitude. He became more loving and affectionate. I told him I can't live without love. I told him I'd had enough. I didn't want to take the initiative all the time. It's really draining, and it just makes me more insecure, having to initiate everything, including sex. I feel like if I didn't do anything, the relationship would fall apart. I don't want to live like that anymore.

Another thing that bothers me is that there is a lot of work to do around the house, but Larry doesn't want to do anything about it. He gets angry when I mention it. We still haven't resolved this, and I don't know what to do about it. I often feel powerless and discouraged. Today is the worst. I just want to go back to bed and forget about things. There is so much to do and I don't know where to start. I feel totally overwhelmed, so I don't do anything. And when things get bad, I turn to drugs. But I don't want to do that anymore. So I guess I just need to accept that things are not the way they should be at the moment. I need to focus on my work, on making an income. Lately I've been drawing on my savings, but there is almost nothing left.

How do I get myself in these predicaments when I should know better, especially at my age? I act like a teenager sometimes. I don't take responsibility, and then I panic. I wish I had a magic wand that could erase all the things that are wrong in my life, starting with this house. There are so many repairs to be done, collapsed patios, leaking taps, overflowing gutters, a garden choked with weeds, a green swimming pool full of leaves and frogs. It's pathetic, but I can't do it on my own. Larry won't listen when I talk to him about it. I just have to let it go, or it will drive me crazy. It will drive me to taking more drugs, and I don't want to do that. I need to put things like the house and other problems out of my mind for the time being, and focus on my health.

22 DECEMBER 2015

YESTERDAY I HAD ANOTHER RELAPSE because I was feeling bad, and I don't know why. I work in mental health now with my new nursing agency, and it's really good because I don't have any access to drugs. Everything is double-checked by two nurses, and all the drugs are accounted for. Every time a drug is used, there is a record of it, and each shift, there is a count of all the schedule four and schedule eight drugs, namely all the ones that can lead to addiction. This is good for me, as I am not tempted to take anything. This is the way it should be. I don't want to be judged for stealing drugs in the past. It's something an addict does, and I am no better than the junkie on the street. I don't feel superior, I'm just better at hiding what I'm doing. Larry hasn't helped me much with this, as he seems to think that I've overcome my problem, but he couldn't be farther from the truth. I have a new strategy though, and I'm confident it will help me.

I need to be 100 percent committed to give up all codeine-based painkillers, no matter what. I always think I'll be able to handle taking them and sticking to the normal dosage, but I'm just kidding myself. Like an alcoholic, I should never pick up the first drink (which in my case is the first tablet), as it will lead to the next one and to the next one. And then it will lead to hurting myself. Addiction is always the same, no matter what the substance is. An alcoholic may persuade himself that he can have a few drinks like everyone else, to be sociable, and then stop. But he can't. It's the same for me. I can't take anything with codeine in it, or I will be back to square one. Maybe these tablets help me suppress something within myself, my feelings, my emotions, all the pain I carry inside.

Even though I have an addiction problem, I know there is also a lot of health in me. I have a burning desire to overcome all of this, to put it behind me. Only a full commitment can achieve this. I did it before, when I gave up drinking. So why can't I do it again? I try to remember how I did it. It was a decision I made, and there was no way back. I decided I would feel better if I didn't drink at all. I've stuck with that resolution ever since, never deviating from it. I know I'll never go back to drinking. I want to make the same decision with codeine painkillers.

The commitment has to be totally waterproof in order to work. No exception, no compromise, no loophole. This is the only way it will work. It has to be 100 percent tight all the time, without fail, no matter what I go through at the time and how crappy I feel. Everyone feels bad from time to time. After all, life is not a rose garden. But things would be much better if I gave up my addiction entirely, without looking back. Then there would be hope—hope that I will feel better. I know I can't take antidepressants; they don't agree with me, and they make me feel worse. This is something I need to handle without chemicals. I can only take herbal products.

Addiction is an entity of its own. It's like an alien taking possession of your body, your mind, all pervasive and cunning. It cajoles you, it talks to you. It wants you to give in to its destructive demands. It constantly messes with your head; that's why you need to be 100 percent committed, or it won't work. The addiction will take advantage of any weakness in you and infiltrate any weak spot, take over your whole thinking, until you can't make sound decisions anymore. It's not about willpower. It's about outsmarting the addiction.

The addiction is like the devil: It wants you to believe crazy lies. It makes it sound harmless. It tells you that you'll be all right, even if you keep taking this substance just once more. It tells you that this time, you'll be able to handle it, but it's not true. You will never be able to handle it. It's as simple as that, or you wouldn't be addicted. You would be able to cope with this like a normal person.

One hundred percent commitment means that my drug of choice is not an option, full stop. It's the only way to stop the constant battle in my head. I have wasted so much precious energy trying to fight this, without any success. Now it's time to put down my weapons and admit that I am powerless. I can't take anything with codeine in it, or it will kill me in the end. Only a 100 percent commitment will work for me. I can't go back, just like when I gave up drinking.

I don't know who I am anymore, what it feels to be normal. I have lost sense of who I really am. I hate the side-effects of these drugs. I used to love how they made me feel, but now it's the opposite. The good feeling, the euphoric high, is very short-lived. Depression soon follows. I hate the anxiety, the racing thoughts and vivid, scary dreams when I try to go to sleep and wake up every hour. I hate it how it makes me feel thirsty and weak the next morning, so depressed I almost feel suicidal. It takes away my joy of living. I used to be a happy person, even though I've always had problems. But there was a kind of resilience in me, and I used to look forward to life.

Now I don't look forward to anything. I feel discouraged, because all my efforts have been in vain. This is why I think the only way is to give up and to resign myself to the fact that I will never ever be able to touch this substance again. It will be easier for me if I do it that way. It's a one-way ticket, with no return. It is *my* choice. Others have done it, and they have healed, so I can do it too.

I need to take things more easily, not so seriously. I get stressed out about stupid things, like cooking dinner for my kids, planning my grocery shopping. I get panicky about the simplest aspects of life. This has to stop. The kids will not starve, after all. They are not babies. Angie is almost ten years old. I can relax. The worst is over. If I want to stop going round and round in circles, I need to stop my addictive behaviour now. Things can only improve once I've done it, once I've made the decision to *live*. God, please help me.

30 DECEMBER 2015

I HAD A RELAPSE ON December 25. I felt so rotten, I couldn't help it. Day three and day five seem to be the worst. Now I am currently at day five. I can feel myself craving this horrible stuff, but I won't give in. I have to be strong and keep going. I took some Valium yesterday, which was prescribed to me a while ago. I took 15 mg and it knocked me out; I had to go to bed early. But at least I didn't relapse. I threw the rest of the tablets down the sink, as I don't want to get addicted to them. I want to feel normal again. I don't even know what that means anymore. All I can feel is this constant fear and depression, and no matter what I do, I can't seem to shake it. I do what I can, exercise, play the piano, do things with Angie, like taking her to the beach.

My friend Melody's husband Lance has been diagnosed with lung cancer, a big shock for both of them, and not a nice Christmas present. He's had radiotherapy already, but they're waiting for an abscess on his lungs to clear with intravenous antibiotics before starting chemotherapy. He's at home, and nurses come to change his IV pump. He has a direct PIC line, so he doesn't need to walk around with an IV pole. The IV pump is kept in a "bum" bag. He's lost twelve kilos already, which actually suits him as he used to be a bit overweight. He's sixty-seven years old, and I hope he will survive. But the problem is he still smokes. Maybe he thinks life is not worth living if he can't smoke.

Sometimes I feel the same, like life is not worth living if I can't have any codeine painkillers. They make me feel so wonderful, so full of energy and enthusiasm. I can do things for hours when I take them. Now I feel empty and discouraged. I don't feel like doing anything, to be honest. I force myself, though. If I do some exercise I'll feel better, so I'll go to the gym.

My older daughter Fiona took the two younger ones with her, Angie and Flynn. They have some work to do at her house, and her partner Rick is good with kids; he has a charismatic personality. He has a sense of humour and is also a handyman. Fiona and Rick recently bought a small house together, but it needs a lot of work. They also became engaged at Christmas. I was over the moon when they told me. This is another reason to be around for a long time and take part in their lives, become involved in the care of their children one day.

I hope Flynn will be able to learn a few things from Rick. Angie won't be able to do much, but at least she'll be off my hands for a while, and I can focus on myself. Going to the gym will be a priority, just to give my body some energy. I feel so stiff and as though all my muscles are hurting, my legs in particular. I've read these are withdrawal symptoms from codeine, and I can believe it. Something to put up with, but I don't want to start all over all the time.

I was told my liver was damaged, and yet I continued taking codeine painkillers. I didn't listen to this warning. I might as well be like Lance, who continues to smoke despite being diagnosed with lung cancer. People judge him for it, and Melody says it breaks her heart, but what I do is not much better. This is the power of addiction. We would rather die than give it up, and yet we cling to life and continue to hope things will improve. We continue to hope there will be light at the end of the tunnel. This is what I am hoping for, and I pray every day that I can do it. I need all the strength, all the perseverance, and all the courage I can muster.

I haven't had much work lately, and money is another thing that continuously worries me. When will this ever change? I am not asking for much, just enough to make ends meet, to pay my bills on time, and to have a regular cash flow. When I take codeine painkillers, I don't worry about anything. It takes everything away, and I can lose myself in the present moment. Why can't I do this without this awful drug? A good way to live is not to worry and to concentrate on the now.

When will I ever learn my lesson? It's nearly the New Year, and when I look back on what I've achieved this year, it isn't much when it comes to my addiction. I thought I'd have beaten it by now, especially after my trip to Europe. I went over three weeks without any codeine, and I felt wonderful. I never once wanted the stuff, or maybe I did once or twice, but I quickly resigned myself that I couldn't have it because I knew it was illegal in Holland, France, and Germany. These countries don't allow codeine-based painkillers of any kind to be sold over the counter.

There is something wrong with the system in Australia. Maybe there is too much greed. The pharmaceutical industry wants to keep making big profits, even if it means putting lives at risk. I wonder how many people are really addicted to codeine and buy large quantities of codeine painkillers every day. Why are the politicians turning a blind eye? They're more interested in lining their pockets than in people dying from an addiction to something that is freely available. I suppose it's a personal choice, to become addicted. You just need to take the proper dosage and follow instructions, and it won't happen.

The truth is hidden from the public, but I'm sure more people die from over-the-counter painkiller overdoses than from heroin or cocaine or even ice overdoses. This stuff is so easy to obtain. I went back many times to the same pharmacies, and they never denied me this drug. They always give it to me. They never ask any questions, except for the standard ones. They never suspect anything, or they turn a blind eye, so the pharmaceutical industry can keep making millions out of people's demise. So much misery: Ordinary people ending up like junkies, craving this stuff like someone on the street looking for a fix. The difference is that this fix is a lot easier to get, and it is totally legal, as well as extraordinarily cheap. A packet of thirty codeine painkiller tablets costs less than $10. It must be the cheapest and most accessible drug ever. How silly to become addicted to something like that, and how embarrassing.

These drugs can do a lot of damage and should be prescription only. People should not be allowed to buy them over the counter. Other countries have implemented this law, so why can't Australia do it too? How many people need to die for things to change?

I plan to continue my diary next year, and hopefully it will only focus on my total recovery. No relapses. Whatever I need to do to get away from this awful substance, I will do it. It's the worst thing that's ever happened to me in my life, but I know I can pull myself out of this mess. My dairy will keep me going.

6 JANUARY 2016

I STARTED THIS YEAR THE wrong way. I didn't even bother making resolutions because I knew I wouldn't follow them anyway. I don't have illusions about myself, and I try not to kid myself anymore. What's the point of lying to yourself, of telling yourself that you will do something, knowing deep down that it won't happen? The truth is that again, I failed at what I set out to do, namely stay away from over-the-counter painkillers.

Today I feel I've reached the end of my tether. I know I've said this many times before, but this time I will do it, no matter what. I won't think about how I feel and that I'm tired and depressed. I will just keep going. It can't be that difficult, after all! If I can give up smoking and drinking without any withdrawal symptoms and without ever looking back, I can do the same with codeine painkillers.

I understand why it should be hard to quit smoking or drinking. Smoking is a social habit, a faithful companion to all your activities, and drinking gives you a nice sensation, this sense of euphoria, of being on top of the world, and sometimes it's good to experience that. It makes you realise the beauty of life, of nature and everything around you.

Codeine painkillers don't do any of these things. Alcohol makes you feel nice. You feel good within yourself, attractive and confident. But codeine makes you doubt yourself. It's a stupid drug, and yet it does so much damage.

I know I've reached my limits with this substance, and I don't enjoy it anymore. I don't even know if I've ever really enjoyed it. There was something self-destructive about taking it, about swallowing handfuls of tablets as if I wanted to kill myself. But I don't want to die. I know this for sure. I don't get any relief from the idea of taking my own life.

I believe I should cling to life. Deep inside of me, there is a person who loves life, and who is a joyful being. I can rediscover this person, this unique being who is in tune with God and the universe, someone who has a strong faith that everything will be all right in the end. I know it will. There is an end to all suffering, and in my case, the end doesn't mean death. It's a new life, a new beginning.

Why has it taken me so long to come to this decision, to give up codeine, my drug of choice, and to do it for good? What's wrong with me? Why couldn't I make up my mind sooner? Don't I have any willpower? I know I'm endangering my health, and yet I keep going back to the chemist to buy more packets of codeine painkillers. What a messed-up person I am! I think I don't want to write anymore in my diary, unless I can talk about something more positive, like my triumph over this addiction. Talking about my relapses is so boring and repetitive. Every time I promise to become clean, I break my promise. The outcome is predictable.

But I don't want this outcome for myself anymore. I want a happy ending, and I know there will be one. This is not an unhappy story. They say there can't be a happy ending to an unhappy story, but in my case, I don't believe I am unhappy. I'm just confused, and I got into a bad habit. Now this habit has taken over my life, but I can get rid of it. Even though my struggle with this substance hasn't ended, I will finish this diary and start a new one.

The new one will focus on my recovery, on being totally clean and never going back to this drug. I know that it is possible, and in my case it's the only choice I have, unless I want to be a junkie lining up for methadone at the chemist every morning. I don't want to be like that. It's not something I can imagine myself doing, but I will have to do it if I don't quit this habit now. I won't have a choice anymore. I will be like all the other junkies, maybe even worse as they seem to be more honest about their addiction. They don't try to hide it like I'm doing.

I feel like a loser, a hypocrite, and yet I want people to think I've got things under control. If only they knew the truth, they would not believe it. They wouldn't like me. This diary is about my struggle. The next diary will be about my recovery. It will be like being reborn. It will be a new life, a new *me*. Or it will be like finding my old me again, the person I lost along the way.

I don't know what will happen, once I find this *real* me. I might want to change my whole life, who knows? When you've lived without your true self for so long, it seems like a huge change, a revolution, something totally different. It would be like being repressed, functioning like a slave or a robot, to becoming human again, with everything it entails. I can't wait to be human again, to be who I'm meant to be.

This will be *my* adventure, and no one will stop me this time, not even me. It's like there are two people living inside of me, the addict and the healthy person. It feels like a battle between the two, but one of them needs to give in, and it's definitely the addict. That lifestyle is not sustainable. The war inside my head needs to come to an end, and there needs to be peace again. I don't want to fight anymore, especially not against myself. If I could just drop my weapons and live in harmony with myself, with my environment, with God, then the need to fight would disappear, and so would the need to take drugs. Every war comes to an end, no matter how long it lasts. There is always an end to it. There is a time for battle, and there is a time for peace.

CONCLUSION

As I go over my diary entries, I notice they're all similar. There is a pattern to my addiction. I always believe that I can do it *on my own*, without any help. And yes, I'm all right for a few days and do what I intend to do until I can't handle things anymore and relapse. My mind talks to me in a treacherous way. It lies to me and wants me to believe I have the power to end this, when in fact I don't.

I've reached the end of my tether. I can't stand myself anymore, and I can't cope with being addicted to codeine painkillers anymore. Sometimes I think about ending my life, like this British police worker who was so lonely and desperate. But I know that's not the solution to my problems. My family needs me, and I have to stay alive for my kids, no matter what. There is no escape. I can't just call it quits by swallowing a cocktail of illegal drugs. There is no end to my suffering unless I give up codeine painkillers.

Maybe I can do some counselling or join a support group. There must be a way I can overcome this terrible addiction, my dirty, shameful secret. My life is out of control. It's a nightmare. Sometimes I wake up at night drenched in sweat, my heart beating furiously. I'm scared out of my mind. I realise what I do to myself, how I hurt my body and destroy my organs by swallowing handfuls of codeine painkillers tablets. It has to end, and the only way is to seek help. I need to get started as soon as possible. No excuses anymore. My next diary will be about becoming totally clean, finally. The game is over. I want to close this door and open a new one. I want to live a new life, a *clean* life. A life of honesty and purpose. A life without codeine painkillers. I pray that I'll have the strength to do it.

Abby Liveringhouse, 5 February 2016